The Desperate Union

What Is Going Wrong in the European Union?

Ewoud van Laer

Translation from Dutch by
Abacus Translation

UNION BRIDGE BOOKS
An imprint of Wimbledon Publishing Company Limited (WPC)

UNION BRIDGE BOOKS
75–76 Blackfriars Road
London SE1 8HA

www.unionbridgebooks.com
Original title: De wanhopige unie

First published: WalburgPers, Zutphen 2017
Copyright © Ewoud van Laer 2017

English translation: Abacus Translation
Copyright © Ewoud van Laer 2020

A CIP record for this book is available from the British Library.

Library of Congress Cataloging-in-Publication Data
Library of Congress Control Number: 2019952778

ISBN-13: 978-1-78527-174-8 (Pbk)
ISBN-10: 1-78527-174-1 (Pbk)

This title is also available as an e-book.

Praise for *The Desperate Union*

This is a remarkable book. It is also an important book because it is about a structural flaw that poses a fatal risk to the monetary union. This flaw is the disregard of the cultural differences that exist within the borders of the European Union. What is remarkable about it is that in addition to official statistics Ewoud van Laer has used detective stories to support his theory. Readers will encounter Inspector Maigret, for example. A well-documented and well-written book.

–Frits Bolkestein, European Commissioner,
1999–2004

While I do not agree with all of Ewoud van Laer's conclusions I found his analysis of the deep cultural and historical roots that separate northern and southern Europe fascinating. His book is essential reading for anyone trying to understand the present deep tensions within the EU.

–Nick Clegg, deputy prime minister of the
United Kingdom, 2010–2016

You need to read this book to understand that Brexit did not come out of nowhere and that we are at a crossroads with regard to the future of our union. Restoring mutual trust by gaining a better understanding of one another's backgrounds would appear to be the solution. Ewoud van Laer provides guidance for this in his book – a 'must read' for anyone who feels involved with the European Union.

–Hans Bartelds, chairman of
Fortis, 1990–2002

I found it very interesting that cultural differences – a topic that many people know about at a general level – have now been set out on paper and examined in depth, illustrated by very relatable and original examples.

–Ina Giscard d'Estaing, chargée de
mission of the Louvre Museum

I have always had my doubts about the monetary union, largely based on my own personal experiences at a great many international meetings. In this book Ewoud van Laer clearly demonstrates the issues we found ourselves wrestling with and how deeply value systems are ingrained in us.

–André Szász, executive director of the
Dutch Central Bank with responsibility for international
monetary relations, 1973–94

In this extremely clearly argued book, Ewoud van Laer demonstrates that we are trapped in a cultural and monetary dilemma. The tenability of the monetary union calls for further integration whilst the priority for people at the moment is maintaining their own way of life. There are no economic models that are able to cope with this dilemma.

–Professor Casper de Vries, Witteveen chair of
Monetary Economics at Erasmus University

It is primarily the combination of hard facts and the examples drawn from literature and real life that make this an important and original book. It transpires that cultural differences are highly significant to the European integration process.

–Edgar du Perron, justice of the Dutch Supreme
Court and professor of Private Law at the
University of Amsterdam

Peace, solidarity and cooperation are only conceivable among peoples and nations who know who they are.

– Václav Havel

CONTENTS

ILLUSTRATIONS

Figures

Tables

FOREWORD

In 1979, the young Ewoud van Laer took his first job at the Dutch Ministry of Finance. Since he was so junior he was soon appointed 'Mr Euro': charged with keeping an eye on the project of European monetary integration, which everyone knew wasn't going to happen anyway.

Decades later, as a fund manager working for stockbrokers and banks, he watched the euro come into existence and swiftly hit trouble. Travelling around Europe, speaking many languages, Van Laer came to feel that the problems weren't simply economic. Beneath the European Union lay a deep but rarely mentioned cultural fault line between north and south. Bizarrely, the divide seemed to track the path of the *limes:* the nearly two-thousand-year-old border that the Romans drew along the Rhine and Danube between their own empire and the unconquered Germanic tribes.

His clear, provocative and commendably brief book tracks this fault line and asks how the EU can live with it. Through an imaginative reading of everything from detective novels to data compiled by international institutions, Van Laer argues that the basic difference between the north and south of the continent is 'power distance'. Northern Europeans tend to treat people, even the boss, more or less as equals; southern Europeans observe strict hierarchies in which the top people cannot be challenged. In Latin countries, the boss is free to break the rules; and the only way the people at the bottom can get what they want is to break them, too.

Van Laer (who identifies unapologetically with northern Europe) argues that power distance creates north–south differences in almost every realm: in employer–employee relations, the independence of judges, willingness to invest in common projects and so on. For centuries now, the cooperative and transparent north has grown faster than the distrustful, hierarchical south. The widening economic divide has created its own difficulties, as witness the tensions over the euro. Northerners feel they are being made to pay for southern indigence. Southerners feel the north has imposed permanent austerity on them.

Ideally, *The Desperate Union* would have appeared in English before the referendum, but now is an excellent moment too. In Britain today, the EU is constantly invoked but poorly understood. The British debate on Brexit tends to assume a monolithic union of mutually indistinguishable 'Europeans'. Van Laer shows what a misconception this is. And rather than treating the United Kingdom as an incompatible non-European outlier, he shows that it falls clearly on the northern European side of the divide. Brexit, it turns out, is not the deepest European fault line.

For now, Brexit is helping to keep the EU together. Britain's floundering since the referendum has encouraged all other member states to keep ahold of nurse for fear of finding something worse. But once Brexit fades into history (if it ever does), the fault line that Van Laer points to might start moving again, and the ensuing earthquake could destroy the EU.

Van Laer advocates reform: let Brussels stick to the things it's good at, such as managing the single market, but stop trying to force north and south to cooperate on divisive issues such as the euro and asylum seekers.

I don't share his views on asylum, immigration and Islam (I'm what he calls 'politically correct') but I only wish our politicians had a smidgen of Van Laer's deep understanding of the contradictory countries that make up the EU. Even now, it's still not too late for Britain's decision-makers to read this book.

Simon Kuper, 9 August 2019
Columnist, the *Financial Times*

INTRODUCTION

CULTURAL DIFFERENCES – WILL THE FRENCH EVER BEHAVE LIKE THE DUTCH?

No two foreigners are alike. Piet Römer, a producer at media company Endemol, believes that Dutch television viewers are more likely to identify with English-language series than with programmes from Latin countries. 'Finding a nice setting is never the problem, what matters to the viewer is the character: can you connect with them? While many Spanish and Italian series are of excellent quality, viewers still find it easier to understand how a character lives and works if they are, say, in New York rather than in Madrid.' Hans Schwartz, head of procurement for the Dutch public broadcaster, makes the same point when he explains why European cooperation in the film industry simply refuses to take off. 'Co-productions often involve making far too many concessions to ensure that all the countries that are contributing financially are given a look-in. The result is a kind of euro pudding.'[1] It would seem that you can't simply mix up the various European national identities. If you do, you get combination characters who behave in a way that makes no sense to anyone: the leader of an Italian mafia clan seeking consensus with his wife, or a French model wearing clogs. Such representations don't make sense to anybody.

I have had similar experiences as a securities investor. I have spent around 40 years travelling the world looking for stocks and bonds offering returns that match the risk appetite of my clients, which include pension funds, charitable organisations and private investors. My professional colleagues and I took our first cautious steps across

---

1 NRC Handelsblad, 24 September 2009.

the border in the 1970s, when the financial sector was still modest in size and had an impeccable reputation. The gap with the English-speaking world was easiest to bridge. Obviously, companies like BP, Coca-Cola and McDonalds were already familiar to us. I can still remember the widespread admiration for the first Dutch pension fund to invest in French government bonds, attracted by the high interest rates. The rest of the sector soon followed suit and before the change of the millennium Dutch savings were being invested all around the world.

I played my own very small part in this globalisation process. Just like the programme buyers, I really tried to understand those foreigners. Sometimes I succeeded, but in hindsight I must conclude that often I failed. I remember visiting the Bank of Italy sometime in the 1990s. Two economists had invited me to lunch. After a glass of wine I risked commenting that the figures for the Italian government deficit were being manipulated. Instead of getting angry or denying it, my hosts smiled genially and said: 'But you know that, right? If your politicians turn a blind eye to it, then surely that means they're OK with it?'

I'm not the only Dutchman to fall into the Italian trap. Nout Wellink, the former president of the Dutch Central Bank, recalls a discussion with his predecessor Wim Duisenberg, who stated: 'We are getting the EMU (Economic and Monetary Union) from 1 January 1999 and, whatever happens, Italy will be a part of it.' Italy was one of the founding members of the European Community. 'In Italy they knew only too well how the figures on Italy's economic performance needed to be constructed in order to meet the convergence criteria'.[2]

We are still unable to watch any Spanish or Italian series, but unlike the film world, financial integration in Europe has proceeded apace. As Duisenberg predicted, we have been inextricably bound to Italy since 1999 because we use the same currency. The euro is not a holiday trip but more like a marriage. The same can be said about other elements of post-war European integration, such as the common external borders, the trade agreements with third countries and the jurisdiction of the European Court of Justice, which supersedes Dutch law.

---

2 Quoted in Marsh (2009), p. 198.

In order to work together successfully in all these fields, we need to understand each other. The question posed in this book is whether we do. Or has the integration process perhaps gone too far? Do we take sufficient account of the fact that the French will never feel like the Dutch and will therefore behave differently? Naturally the same applies to Germans, Italians and the residents of all those countries we have become so closely connected to. And what do they think about us? Do they laugh at us because they think we are too trusting, as happened to me at the Bank of Italy?

I cannot stand the fact that misconceptions such as these play no role whatsoever in the debates on European integration. Politicians and their advisers act as if the measures imposed by Brussels have the same effects on the citizens of the various countries. This is not the case. My purpose in writing this book is to show the consequences of the profound cultural differences in Western Europe.

We begin with a description of the post-war integration process. This is followed in Chapter 2 with some examples of cooperation within various important institutions in 13 Western European countries. Western Europe is meant in the broad sense: from Greece in the south to Norway in the north of the continent.[3] I refer to the well-known research by the World Economic Forum (WEF) into the competitive position of these countries. In doing so, my emphasis is not on quantitative differences, such as inflation and the wage costs which are cited in many publications. I am mainly interested in the less tangible, qualitative aspects that influence a country's competitive strength in the long term, such as the scale of corruption, the way in which employers and employees cooperate and how people treat each other in the workplace. Research shows that – as we all know – there is no such thing as a perfect country. Crooks and bullies are found everywhere, but the degree to which such behaviour is tolerated varies from country to country. Some countries differ considerably, others only by degrees.

To illustrate my points I cite as many eyewitnesses as possible. In addition I quote examples from detective stories, current affairs and scientific research. The genre of the detective story, a British

---

3 Belgium and Switzerland are largely disregarded because of the mixed cultural nature of these countries.

invention, has conquered the world in recent decades. Because murder
constitutes the violation of a universal fundamental right, these books
and films about the adventures of various sleuths can in principle be
understood both within their country of origin and beyond. However,
the way in which the perpetrator is tracked down and brought to
justice differs from country to country. These differences allow me to
demonstrate how the same problem is tackled in different countries.

The examples illustrate how behaviour in various Western
European countries can be very different. Is this down to the random
examples I present, or do all Dutch, Spanish and Germans tend to
act in the same way? We will discuss this question in Chapter 3, in
which I present various findings of game theoretical research. Game
theory is a branch of science that studies how groups of people
cooperate with one another and reach decisions. In this case we are
dealing with the so-called public goods games, in which participants
invest in a joint project to allow it to grow and flourish. We could
think of the real-life examples of the single internal market of the
European Union (EU) or maintaining the euro. These studies show
that in some countries cooperation is encouraged if there is a possibility to punish free-riders, while in other countries this proves to be
counterproductive.

I believe that the reason for the differences discovered lies in the
wide range of value systems. It would seem that ideas about right and
wrong differ from one country to another. Because of this, a certain
event will trigger different feelings and different behaviour among the
citizens of different countries. In Chapter 4 I report on the study
by social psychologist Geert Hofstede on cultural differences. Various
examples from the past show that the differences in the countries
considered have existed for centuries and are therefore deeply rooted
in our national personalities. The consequences of this feed through
into our modern-day political and economic lives. Chapter 5 takes a
closer look at the difficult period the EU is currently going through.
A majority of the electorate in the United Kingdom expressed the
wish to leave the EU, a scenario that could be repeated in other
countries.

My aim in writing this book is to see to it that cultural differences
start playing a part in the debate about further European integration.
Every European is aware of these differences, but when agreements

are being made and treaties signed it is implicitly assumed that all member states are equally willing and able to implement these. By now it is quite clear that this is not the case. To prevent European cooperation from suffering irreparable damage in the coming years we would be wise, as the closing chapter demonstrates, to take a step back with regard to the common labour market, the asylum policy and the monetary union.

Chapter 1

NO MORE WAR

The origins of today's Western European political and economic integration go back to the devastation of the Second World War. The German author and artist Günter Grass, who was taken prisoner of war as a 17-year-old conscript, wrote in his autobiography: 'From the moment I was behind barbed wire, I was hungry. But what I really should say is that hunger occupied me like an empty house.'[1] At this point most Germans were even worse off. The British occupying authorities allowed a ration of 1,550 calories a day for 'normal' consumers. However, in Hamburg provisions did not get above 1,206 calories a day.[2] And that meant being hungry all the time.

The situation was equally dire in the Netherlands and Belgium. When Arthur Muttah, the protagonist in *The Tears of the Acacias* by Dutch novelist Willem Frederik Hermans, is given a lift by his Canadian liberators in the spring of 1945, he sees a ruined country.

> At times it seemed as if the car was driving over a low dam through a lake. Sometimes the water was so high that it covered the road and you could hear it sloshing against the bottom of the cargo box [...] Beyond Amersfoort the country was largely dry again. But sometimes all that was left of a farm was its chimney.

In Belgium things were little better. 'On the other side of the canal whole rows of houses had collapsed. Green trams jingled along with sheets of cardboard instead of windows. Many homes had been boarded up with wood or cardboard.'[3]

---

1 Grass (2008), p. 181.
2 Rademacher (2003), pp. 80/1.
3 Hermans (1971), pp. 232, 235.

Things were not quite as desperate in Paris, judging by the description given by French author Simone de Beauvoir.

Transportation was in chaos; there was a shortage of food, coal, gas and electricity. When it got cold, Sartre wore an old, threadbare lumber jacket. One of his prison camp friends sold me a rabbit coat that kept me warm; but, except for a black suit that I kept for special occasions, I had only the oldest of clothes to put on underneath, and I continued wearing shoes with wooden soles.' And so she was in for a shock when she visited the Netherlands in November 1946. 'Everyone talked about the famine. The parks were stripped bare; all the trees had been chopped down to fill the fireplaces […] The country was taking a long time to recover; in the shop-windows only "ersatz" products were displayed; the big department stores were empty and I came back to Paris with my pockets full of florins I hadn't managed to spend.

The situation in Berlin, which Simone visited some months after that, was much worse again. 'I felt very uneasy getting on the train to Berlin. The idea of seeing Germans and talking to them was painful […] As soon as I set foot in Berlin I found my bitterness disarmed. Everything was in ruins; so many cripples and so much poverty! Alexanderplatz, Unter den Linden, everything had been smashed to pieces […] We talked to some students; no books, not even in the libraries; nothing to eat, the cold.'[4]

However, the greatest damage wreaked on this part of the world by the Second World War was not material but psychological. Günter Grass described the denazification process at his prison camp.

The American 'education officer', with his spectacles and soft voice and freshly ironed shirts, did not get very far with us; we, myself included, refused to believe the evidence he put before us, the black-and-white pictures of Bergen-Belsen, Ravensbrück […] I saw piles of corpses, the ovens […] 'You mean Germans did that?' we kept asking. 'Germans could never have done

---

4 Beauvoir (1977), pp. 18, 132, 162–63.

that.' And among ourselves we said: 'Propaganda. Pure propaganda.'[…] It was some time before I came gradually to understand and hesitantly to admit that I had unknowingly – or, more
precisely, unwilling to know – taken part in a crime that did not
diminish over the years and for which no statute of limitations
would ever apply, a crime that grieves me still. Guilt and the
shame it engendered can be said, like hunger, to gnaw, gnaw
ceaselessly. Hunger I suffered only for a time, but shame.

Grass was to experience even greater anguish after he found out
what had happened to his mother during this period. 'Not once during
the few years she had left did my mother so much as drop a hint or
utter a word that might indicate what had gone on in the empty shop,
in the basement, or in the apartment, nothing that might indicate
where and how often she had been raped by Russian soldiers […]
Nor could I bear to come out with things long lurking within me: the
questions I had failed to ask […] my petrified faith […] the Hitler
Youth campfires […] my desire to die a hero's death like Lieutenant
Commander Prien of the submarines – and as a volunteer.'[5]
Like most French people, Simone de Beauvoir was not
tormented by guilt. Her description is very matter-of-fact. 'Those
who had been deported returned and we discovered that we had
known nothing. The walls of Paris were covered with photographs
of charnel houses'. Ordinary life resumed without much trouble.
'In June [1945] the Prix de la Pléiade was awarded for the second
time. I was invited to take coffee with the members of the jury, who
were all assembled at a luncheon at Gallimard's […] There were a
great many people, bright sunlight, champagne, gin and plenty of
whisky.' A few weeks later she decided to go on a bicycling holiday.
'It was still difficult to find food and lodging; we had brought some
canned American food with us which came in very handy for filling
up after meals. We slept in back of a baker's shop, on café benches,
and once we even slept in a charcoal burner's hut, practically in the
open air.'[6]

---

5 Grass (2008), pp. 219–20, 320.
6 Beauvoir (1975) pp. 40, 43–44.

What would Günter Grass not have given to exchange his troubles for those of Simone de Beauvoir! Even so, like almost all Europeans, both had been deeply affected by the horrors of recent years and everyone had the same deeply held desire: No more war!

That was easy enough to say, but how could this objective, this deeply held feeling, be realised? In September 1945, after peace had also been formally declared in the Far East, the Americans stopped the aid programmes to their European allies. It quickly became clear that they had done so too soon: economic recovery ground to a halt and Russian influence in the political life of all European countries increased. In light of these developments, the Americans decided to slow down their withdrawal. In 1947, US Secretary of State George Marshall launched his European Recovery Program. All countries that had been affected by the war were offered sizeable loans in US dollars to enable them to fund the imports needed for reconstruction. It was also a way for the Americans to encourage their European allies to lower their import tariffs and thus boost international trade.

Viewing the move as a bid to expand US influence, the Soviet leader Josef Stalin refused the aid being offered – not just for his own country but also blocking what became known as Marshall Aid to other Eastern European countries. This was the origin of the Iron Curtain which was to divide the European continent until 1989. The battle between the two superpowers was mainly fought out in Germany. In the immediate post-war years the two parties, with Great Britain and France in a subordinate role, implemented agreements aimed at obtaining war reparations from the defeated Germany and dismantling its production facilities. The policy was designed to prevent the Germans from manufacturing not only weapons but also other goods needed to wage war, such as heavy machinery, radio transmitting equipment and chemicals. However, the policy also prevented the Germans from earning any foreign currency with which to pay off their war debts. Fearing food riots, the British occupation authorities started importing bread to Germany from the United Kingdom. According to British calculations, the United Kingdom received two million pounds in war reparations in the first year of occupation while Germany received over 100 million pounds worth of food aid.[7]

---

7 Wasserstein (2008), p. 482.

No wonder that the United Kingdom, where bread and many other goods were still rationed, was keen to end this policy. The Americans backed the policy change and in December 1947 the decision was taken to extend Marshall Aid to Germany.

This decision by the Anglo-Saxon allies displeased not just the Russians but also the French. They wanted the war reparations to continue, not just in the form of cash but also of agricultural and mining products and the employment of German workers in France. In addition, they wanted to establish a customs union with the Saarland region and a buffer state on the left bank of the Rhine. However, power relations being what they were, the French did not have much choice but to accept the integration of Germany into Western Europe. To prevent the emergence of a new dictator it was proposed to make the new Germany a decentralised state. In February 1948, a democratic, federative structure was chosen and in June of that year a new central bank was established and a new currency, the Deutschmark, introduced. The communiqué from the military governors was crystal clear. The new bank 'will not be subject to domination by the state [...] It will therefore be possible to avoid many of the undesirable monetary and credit policies followed by German central banks in the past'.[8] The following year a new constitution was adopted and elections were held, and Konrad Adenauer took office as the first chancellor of the Federal Republic of Germany. With Russia blocking these changes in its occupation zone, the new Germany was split into West and East Germany.

What could be done, in this new political constellation, to prevent Germany from once again becoming the most powerful nation on the European continent? This issue was considered by French experts in particular. On 9 May 1950, the French foreign minister Robert Schuman launched a revolutionary plan. He proposed that

'Franco-German production of coal and steel as a whole be placed under a common High Authority, within the framework of an organisation open to the participation of the other countries of Europe [...] This production will be offered to the world as a whole [...] with the aim of contributing to raising living standards and to promoting peaceful achievements [...] In this way, there will be realised simply

_____

8 Marsh (2009), p. 34.

and speedily that fusion of interest which is indispensable to the establishment of a common economic system; it may be the leaven from which may grow a wider and deeper community between countries long opposed to one another by sanguinary divisions.'[9]

This European Coal and Steel Community (ECSC) enabled the French government to monitor the two production sectors that were essential to any rearmament drive by Germany. In addition, it provided a framework for European cooperation. The objectives were clear: peace and prosperity. In order to achieve these, cooperation would be developed in two strategic sectors and the door was opened to 'a wider and deeper community'. Other sectors would follow in the subsequent decades. Schuman also outlined the basic model of the institutional structure. In addition to an executive committee consisting of civil servants (the High Authority), a special council would be set up in which politicians of the participating countries would have a seat. Finally, there would be a common assembly with an advisory role, and a court of justice to settle disputes. These institutions were to form the blueprint for the current institutional structure of the European Union (EU).

France and Germany, the latter embracing the plan with open arms as a way of ending its isolation, were joined by the Netherlands, Belgium, Luxembourg and Italy as founding members of the new community. The United Kingdom, where Winston Churchill had been re-elected prime minister in 1951, did not join. The country still considered itself a global player, largely on the strength of the Commonwealth and its 'special relationship' with the United States. As a result of this choice France became the dominant player in continental Western Europe.

Following a difficult start amid the ruins of the Second World War, European integration became a success story. An important step was taken in 1957 when the government leaders of the six member states agreed in Rome to eliminate customs duties on internal trade in all goods and services over the next 10 years. After the agreements on coal and steel, the French wanted special regulations for agriculture. Guaranteed prices were agreed on a wide range of products including wine, butter, olive oil and sugar beets to protect the farming

---

9 www.robert-schumann.eu/en/ declaration-of-9-may-1950.

community from the effects of the free market. In March 1969, not long after the full abolition of internal trade tariffs, President De Gaulle explained to the then German chancellor Kiesinger why agriculture was so important to his country.

> France has a certain hesitancy and caution regarding Germany's economic strength [...] Germany has been a large industrialised country for a long time. As a result, with its entrepreneurs, its population and its infrastructure it is best equipped for production, trade and especially export [...] France went into the phase of large-scale industrialisation much later. It has been an agricultural country for much longer, with far fewer large cities and large corporations [...] In industry and trade Germany is in the lead.[10]

De Gaulle was proved right: the Germans more than recouped the agricultural subsidies – largely paid for by them – with the sale of their industrial products to France and the other member states. Trade barriers are not only created by the levy of import duties but can also result from a difference in product standard requirements in the respective countries. Since then, thousands of directives and decrees have been issued describing these product requirements in minute detail in order to develop a properly functioning internal market where manufacturers can sell their goods to their European neighbours just as easily as at home – the so-called level-playing field. This can lead to ludicrous situations, such as the ban on green beach flags on the grounds that these could suggest 'that it is safe to swim, while danger can always be present' and the inability to ban plastic shopping bags. But in many cases the consumer benefits, as with the standardisation of plugs and sockets and mobile phone chargers.

As well as the increase in internal trade, the growing number of countries still lining up to join the EU – as the successor to the ECSC is now known – is an indication of its success. The United Kingdom was the first to apply for membership in 1961, having realised by then that more of the country's prosperity was contributed by trade with continental Western Europe than with its (former) colonies. In the

---

10 Quoted in Marsh (2009), p. 49.

nine years since the ECSC had been established, the combined economies of the six member states had grown twice as fast as the UK
economy (58 per cent versus 27 per cent).[11] But, reluctant to share his
position of power with his former rival, President De Gaulle vetoed
the UK's accession. The process was repeated in 1967, but two years
later, with De Gaulle off the scene, the United Kingdom saw its
chance and joined the successful European Economic Community
(EEC), as it was called at the time, along with Ireland and Denmark,
with effect from 1973. At the end of the war, the UK economy had
been larger than that of France and Germany combined, but by 1973
it was lagging behind, having been overtaken by the West German
economy in 1955 and by France in 1970.

Other countries followed. In the 1980s, the 'Europe of the nine'
was expanded with Greece, Spain and Portugal, followed in the 1990s
by Sweden, Finland and Austria. Twelve Eastern European countries
joined in the first decade of the new millennium. And there is no
shortage of interest in becoming a member of the EU, with countries
such as Serbia, Ukraine and Turkey eager to join.

In the early 1970s, European integration gained a new dimen-
sion with the demise of the global fixed exchange rate system. From
now on exchange rates would be determined by the free market.
This development was bad news for the European trade bloc
because while entrepreneurs were able to sell their goods in the other
member states without being hampered by import duties or differing
product requirements, they now ran the risk of being impacted by
exchange rates pricing their goods out of the market. And so in April
1972, the nine partners agreed to limit the fluctuations between their
respective currencies in what was called a 'snake arrangement'. It
was not long-lived; with international investors having a clear preference for the Deutschmark, the German currency appreciated against
the other snake currencies. Within a year, the British pound, the
Italian lira and the French franc had withdrawn from the system. In
1979, another attempt was made at stabilising the mutual exchange
rates with the establishment of the European Monetary System.
But it soon became clear that the Deutschmark retained its tendency to appreciate against the other member currencies in the new

---

11 Maddison (2003), table 1b for this and subsequent calculations.

system. Despite this, in 1999, the decision was taken to introduce a single common currency, the euro. This was a pretty risky move considering that since 1972 the German currency had appreciated by 10 per cent against the Dutch guilder (i.e. on average 0.4 per cent per annum), by over 50 per cent against the French franc (2.7 per cent per annum) and by around 80 per cent against the lira and peseta (5–6 per cent per annum).

In 1985, the objective of free movement of goods, services and capital was supplemented with the Schengen Agreement on the free movement of people. The six original member states were the initial signatories to the treaty, which proposed to gradually allow free movement of people across internal borders over the next years and to maintain a common external border. The number of countries participating increased in the following years and measures were introduced to regulate the influx of asylum seekers. The Dublin Regulation determined that asylum must be requested in the country that was the first point of entry to the Schengen area.

'No more war' was a desire deeply held by the entire European population after the Second World War. Gradually, the understanding grew that European integration was a way of achieving this objective. The approach has obviously been a successful one. Internal conflict has ended. Who could imagine waging war against Germany or France ever again? Furthermore there has been a phenomenal rise in prosperity, we have more leisure time than ever before and we are better educated and healthier than our parents and grandparents. So it is no wonder that up until recently the never-ending flow of integration measures met with barely any resistance from EU citizens.

Now this positive stance can no longer be taken for granted. Successive euro crises and the mass influx of immigrants have led large sections of the population to question whether Europe is still on the right track. Will the Greeks ever pay off their debt? Are there enough jobs for immigrants or will they be on benefits for the rest of their lives? Many politicians and commentators dismiss such criticism as populism. 'We are going to help these people' is the politically correct attitude and 'further European integration is how we are going to do it'. If a large proportion of the population feel that their concerns are not being heard, the EU will see its popularity dwindle further over the next years. Legitimate questions deserve serious answers. I will revert to this in the concluding chapter. But first let's take a look at the cultural differences between the countries of Western Europe and the impact these have on their political and economic functioning.

Chapter 2

WORKING TOGETHER

In a detective story, a crime is committed, which is resolved as the plot unfolds. The quest is conducted by the hero of the story: a private eye, a police inspector or a lawyer. The popularity of the genre shows that many people are attracted to this style of narrative. The genre does not set out to give a realistic representation of a murder inquiry but rather to tell a convincing, exciting story populated by characters that the reader can identify with. This means that a crime novel will only be successful if it gives an accurate portrayal of the society in which the story is set. By comparing detectives, we are also able to compare countries.

For our purposes, solving the murder ('whodunnit') is less important than the sidetracks that say something about how people cooperate in the country where the story is set. Is there corruption in evidence? Do class differences play a role? How do people treat each other in the workplace? Comparing detective stories from different countries can give us a sense of the differences between these countries.

To assess whether the examples from fictitious stories are not random or coincidental but instead an accurate reflection of normal conduct in these countries, I supplement these examples with real-life cases and with the findings of scientific research. Renowned institutions such as the World Bank, the IMD business school and the World Economic Forum have developed objective benchmarks to assess various developments in individual countries on an annual basis. Let's start with corruption.

Corruption among Government Employees

Corruption in Germany

It is the evening of Wednesday, 4 January 2012, and the whole of Germany is glued to the television (see Table 2.1). Federal President Christian Wulff is being questioned about whether he, as reported in *Bild* newspaper, accepted a loan of more than 500,000 euros in 2008 from businessman Egon Geerkens to buy his home in the village of Grossburgwedel near Hanover. The affair escalated after it was revealed that Wulff phoned the editorial team of *Bild* shortly before the date of publication to threaten them with criminal proceedings. This is not just about corruption but also about freedom of the press. The public have their doubts. Before *Bild* launched its campaign against the German president, the vast majority of people were impressed with the flamboyant way in which Wulff and his attractive wife Bettina performed their duties. But in the run-up to the television interview public opinion shifted and now roughly half the population considers that Wulff should resign.[1] Comments made by Wulff

Table 2.1 Corruption among government employees (10 = customary, 0 = never)

Denmark	9.29
Sweden	8.87
Norway	8.58
The Netherlands	8.44
United Kingdom	8.15
Germany	8.15
Ireland	8.01
Austria	7.58
Average	*7.33*
France	7.15
Portugal	6.29
Spain	5.72
Greece	4.58
Italy	4.43

Source: World Economic Forum; average scores from the Global Competitiveness Reports, 2006–15 (inclusive).

1 www.Infratest-dimap.de, February 2012.

during the interview such as 'I would not like to be president of a country where you can no longer borrow money from a friend' do him no favours in Germany.

In the weeks following the interview, journalists start digging deeper and turn up some interesting results. It turns out that on several occasions Bettina Wulff has worn expensive clothes by German fashion designers without paying. This benefit was, however, included in her tax return.[2] Cars emerge as another sensitive issue. In 2010, Wulff leased a Skoda Yeti at 1 per cent of the retail price instead of the customary 1.5 per cent – a saving of 100 euros a month. A year later the couple is able to drive an Audi Q3 free of charge before the model is even on the market. And then there are the holiday homes, luxury plane trips and overnight stays around the October beer festival in Munich – all reinforcing the impression that the Wulffs find it hard to draw a clear line between business and private interests.

A majority of the German population considers this behaviour unacceptable and thinks that Wulff should step down.[3] When the court in Hannover strips him of his political immunity on 16 February, just six weeks after the television interview, Christian Wulff steps down as federal president. The court of justice decides not to let matters rest and launches criminal proceedings against Wulff on the grounds of acceptance of benefits. Following a two-year preparation period, during 22 days of hearings no fewer than 45 witnesses are called, including bodyguards, hotel staff and former employees. To no avail. In February 2014, the former federal president is acquitted of corruption and awarded damages. Despite this, 67 per cent of the population believes he was right to step down. Only 22 per cent of those questioned regret the way things were handled.[4] Even when the affair was at its height, weekly *Der Spiegel* wrote: 'Here is someone who is living in two worlds, with two different value systems. There is the world of the Wulffs [...] and the rest of the world, where people must abide by the letter of the law or lose their job [...] Why should the same not apply to the head of state as is required of the man in the street?'[5]

---

2 www.spiegel.de, 6 January 2012.
3 www.infratest-dimap.de, February 2012.
4 www.spiegel.de, Forsa-Umfrage, 17 June 2014.
5 *Der Spiegel* 6/2012, p. 31.

In a country that has such a collective aversion to corruption it is not easy to find a crime novel dealing with this topic. In his Self trilogy, former judge Bernhard Schlink tests the boundaries of what is – and what is not – acceptable. The hero of these stories is Gerhard Self, a former public prosecutor during the Nazi era. After 1945 there is no longer a place for him in the judiciary and he keeps his head above water by working as a private detective. The third part of the trilogy, entitled *Self's Murder*, sees Self setting a trap for some child abductors. He is assisted by his friend, the recently retired police commissioner Nägelsbach. They act outside of the official channels. The plan fails, shots are fired, Nägelsbach is wounded and someone is even killed. However, the police turn a blind eye to the friends' involvement. In hospital Nägelsbach starts to feel remorse for his involvement in this private initiative.

> 'You won't understand me,' Nägelsbach gave us an apologetic look, 'but I don't want to keep the police out of it. I have always had a clear conscience and been on the right side of the law.' 'What does your wife think?' 'She thinks', he flushed, 'she says my soul is at stake. And that she and I must accept the consequences and that if the worst comes to the worst she will look for a job [...] Surely I can't spend my whole life seeing to it that people pay for their crimes and then all of a sudden myself.'

Unlike Christian Wulff, the former police commissioner does not wish to apply double standards, the rules that apply to other offenders apply to him, too. His wife shares his opinion. A prison sentence with a clear conscience is preferable to living in freedom with gnawing self-reproach.

Later on, Self discovers that his client is in fact the murderer he has been hunting. When he threatens to get away, Self also faces a crisis of conscience. 'My powerlessness seared my guilt at S's death into my mind, and forever sealed that neither as a public prosecutor nor a private detective had I left behind anything I could be truly proud of. It consumed me like a rage, a fear, a pain, an insult. I had to do something if I didn't want it to devour me entirely.'[6] Self considers killing

---

6 Schlink (2009), p. 560.

the perpetrator himself and accepting the consequences, but this plan is thwarted by a heart attack. Once recovered, he realises that he will have to learn to live with this unsatisfactory outcome. 'This decision was mine. So I did my best.'[7] Germans take tough action against offenders as a nation, and a violation of rules that apply to everyone also affects them personally at an emotional level. Nägelsbach and Self are both prepared to make considerable sacrifices in return for the peace of mind that results from a clear conscience.

Corruption in Spain

The world of Spanish football is no stranger to scandal. Sometimes even distinguished elderly gentlemen are arrested, as happened to Josep Lluis Núñez, who was president of FC Barcelona for over 20 years. This one-time building contractor was sentenced to six years in prison for a series of corrupt dealings, including bribery of tax inspectors. Three years later, the Spanish Supreme Court reduced his sentence to two years and two months. FC Barcelona is by no means the only Spanish football club to engage in such practices. In 2002, Fiorentino Pérez, the president of Real Madrid, saw an opportunity to pay off the club's 177-million-euro debt by selling the club's training ground to the province. The sum that the province subsequently received for the five skyscrapers built on the site was considerably smaller than the 290 million euros it had paid to the club. Many other football clubs have also engaged in property transactions of this type, along with tax fraud and other illegal actions. Corruption also occurs at other public and private institutions. A 2014 study by Institut d'Economia de Barcelona looks at corruption scandals at lower levels of government.[8] In most cases, these involve kickbacks paid to local politicians by building companies in exchange for changes to land use plans. The research shows that scandals of this type during local elections mainly influence independent voters who do not belong to a political party. Voters like this become demoralised if such practices occur repeatedly and demonstrate this by refraining from voting. By contrast, core supporters on both sides of the political

---

7 Ibid., pp. 625, 632.
8 Solé-Ollé and Sorribas-Navarro (2014) and Costas-Pérez (2014).

spectrum remain loyal to their own candidates, even after they have been exposed. In other words, corruption carries no electoral penalty. So, then why should corrupt mayors and aldermen change the way they operate? Pablo Iglesias, the leader of the successful, recently established political party Podemos, describes how things work in his country. 'These families, whose surnames are all still familiar to us, have all become accustomed to the fact that if you want to get rich in Spain you don't need to be intelligent or have a good nose for business, all you need is to be close to where the power is.'[9] Corrupt entrepreneurs, bankers and senior officials play an important role in the work of popular author Manuel Vázquez Montalbán. In his own country this literary all-rounder is most famous as the creator of detective Pepe Carvalho. As a true Catalonian, Montalbán is a passionate supporter of FC Barcelona. In the story *Off Side*, local football club Centellas is languishing towards the bottom of the league, despite its illustrious past. By coincidence the club's ground is located in a spot which is crucial to the future expansion of the city. The president of Centellas secured his position thanks to the support of Basté de Linyola, president of the mighty FC Barcelona. This former mayor of the city, along with several building contractors, has set his sights on the Centellas ground with a view to selling it on to the municipality at a profit. Their plan is to force the club to sell up by seeing to it that the first team is relegated, plunging the club into financial difficulties. However, when the team defies expectations by winning a number of games, Basté starts having doubts about the plan. He discusses his concerns with his lawyer.

> Time is short. An agreement on a new development plan for the Centellas pitch is only interesting from a business perspective if no one knows that such an agreement will ever happen […] I don't trust that president.' 'He stands to gain the most. He knows that the reason we made him president of Centellas was to make this happen […] He is a man with a short neck who attacks with his head. Remember the file I compiled about his activities, particularly the section on smuggling photo material in the 1960s and the hookers he frequented until he discovered

9 *Financial Times*, 28 November 2015.

the massage parlours.' 'I didn't look at it.' 'But keep it in a safe place. I don't think it will be necessary for you to make it public, I can do that, but he will fight back and while he knows a few things about me, he knows nothing about you. In fact, nobody knows anything about you.

After Pepe Carvalho has got to the bottom of the fraud surrounding the football club, including a murder, he arrives at a sobering assessment of the people who run his city. 'Basté used philosophy and Camps poetry, but they were both criminals, two purebred white criminals, with connections to all the other purebred white criminals, who were even more difficult to spot at the police stations than the Arabs and the blacks. So difficult, in fact, that nobody even bothered to identify them.'[10]

That is how the system works. The business partners are aware of the fact that the other parties hold evidence of their offences. Knowing that bringing a charge against someone else will lead directly to their own downfall, no one would dream of denouncing an accessory. Basté is the only one who falls outside this system because he is untouchable. As such he is the *capo di tutti capi*. Detective Carvalho realises this but can see no way of ending the rule of an elite who are forced by the system of cronyism to protect one another in this way.

Conclusion

Table 2.1 shows that corruption occurs in all Western European countries. After digesting the stories from Spain and Germany we now have an impression of the differences between these countries. Both detectives succeed in exposing the culprits, but the Spaniard Carvalho, who is angry about the state of affairs, has no choice but to resign himself to the existing power relations. Just like many real-life rulers, Basté and his cronies enjoy too much political protection to be charged. The Germans Self and Nägelsbach experience the same emotions but do have a choice: to involve the official authorities or not. The fact that both choose the latter option does not detract from the fact that the German system functions in principle. This conclusion

---

10 Vázquez Montalbán (2012), pp. 201, 207, 262–63.

is confirmed by the forced resignation of Federal President Christian Wulff on account of a few modest financial benefits.

The principle of legal equality is known in both countries but there are considerable differences in how it is applied, both in fictional crime novels and in the reality of presidents, mayors and entrepreneurs. In contrast to Germany, the elites in Spain would often appear to have more power than the official authorities. This means that there is less chance of corrupt politicians and businesspeople being punished in Spain. Ultimately, this difference is due to the differing levels of acceptance of such behaviour by the general public.

Relations between Employers and Employees

Labour Relations in France

On 5 October 2015, a board meeting was taking place at the Air France offices at Charles de Gaulle airport to discuss the increasingly pressing need to cut costs. For the first time ever, compulsory redundancies were on the table (see Table 2.2). Nothing unusual so far; the topic had been high on the agenda of former state-owned companies

Table 2.2 Relations between employers and employees (1 = hostile, 10 = cooperative)

Denmark	8.57
Norway	8.15
Austria	8.15
The Netherlands	8.15
Sweden	8.01
Ireland	7.44
Germany	7.29
United Kingdom	7.29
Average	*6.95*
Portugal	6.01
Spain	6.01
Greece	5.29
Italy	5.15
France	4.86

Source: World Economic Forum; average scores from the Global Competitiveness Reports, 2006–15 (inclusive).

around the world for many years. However, this meeting was to become notorious for the images that appeared on internet the very same day. A group of angry employees stormed a fence and took control of the boardroom where the managers were meeting. Amid the large group of demonstrators with banners and flags it was difficult to make out exactly what happened, but a short while later it was clear that some managers had been physically assaulted. Human resources manager Xavier Broseta was in a particularly bad way, losing not only his glasses but also his jacket and shirt. He escaped his attackers by fleeing and scaling a fence, still wearing his tie but minus his shirt. One union leader later said that Broseta had 'narrowly escaped being lynched'.[11]

The incident was not only a disgrace for France, with the whole world sniggering over the images on YouTube, but also a blow to François Hollande. Two weeks after the events at Air France the Socialist president, who, during the 2012 presidential campaign, still had the backing of the trade unions, called a high-level meeting with the social partners. As soon as it was announced that a number of members of the Charles de Gaulle Trade union were to be prosecuted for what had happened at Air France the union announced it would stay away from the meeting. This was particularly regrettable given that the same meeting the previous year had been boycotted by no fewer than three unions.

Where was all this anger and unwillingness to consult on the part of the employees and their representatives coming from? The government had given in to all their demands: compulsory redundancies at Air France had been whisked off the table, protesting Normandy farmers had been granted higher prices for their products, Parisian taxi drivers had succeeded in limiting the competition from Uber and judges were no longer being pressured to reform the way they were organised. For decades successive administrations, on both the left and the right of the political spectrum, had caved in before a serious debate had even started. The golden rule of survival in French politics was evidently not to resist angry mobs. Aurélie Boullet, a civil servant with the Aquitaine region, had an explanation for the fraught labour relations in her

---

11 www.bbc.co.uk/news/business-34505548.

country. Under the pseudonym Zoé Shepard, she published her book *Absoluement dé-bordée!* (which could be translated as *Absolutely Swamped!*) about her experiences working for the provincial government. She summarised her analysis – which, judging by the sales figures, was widely supported – as follows:

> France is swarming with people in managerial positions who owe their job to a political friend. Pure political clientelism: a well-paid job as a way of rewarding someone for services rendered so that you can rely on them at the next municipal, regional or provincial elections. Political appointments lead to unnecessary costs for the community, because that friend who is made the boss of something they don't know the first thing about means that a new manager needs to be hired. At the same time that person, who has thus become completely superfluous, is obviously not going anywhere.[12]

Telecom billionaire and self-made man Xavier Niel told the *Financial Times* about the mindset of this kind of elite. 'You went to the same school. Your parents knew each other. On all these paths, you've been among yourselves. And among yourselves, nobody wants to upset anyone' Most French business leaders 'are heirs, who frequent the same circles, or were given their posts directly or indirectly by the political powers. Then there's a very egotistical remuneration. And they generally don't create great things.'

Of the scandals that regularly hit this group, he said: 'They think that if you make the rules, you're not subject to them.'[13]

The same attitude can be seen right up to the very highest level. President Mitterrand got into trouble with contaminated blood, Chirac magicked fictitious jobs, Sarkozy boosted his campaign funds with forbidden gifts, Hollande was embarrassed by the tax-evasion antics of his budget minister and Macron had barely been sworn in as president when four ministers were forced to resign after accusations of fraud and corruption.

---

12 *Het Financieele Dagblad*, 28 September 2015.
13 *Financial Times*, 4 May 2013.

The national elite, which has loyally served successive presidents, live and work in Paris and tend to have been schooled in the typically French system of the *grandes écoles*. The most famous of these elite institutes is the École Nationale d'Administration (ENA), founded by De Gaulle shortly after of the Second Word War. It was not without reason that the father of the nation called the students 'an elite in every respect, an intellectual elite, a moral elite'.[14] Such utterances are awkward for the present-day boards of ENA and other *grandes écoles* such as the École Polytechnique and the École Normale Supérieure. The elitist cachet sits uncomfortably with the modern view that talent should come before background. Nevertheless, director of admissions at the Polytechnique Michel Godin acknowledged that 70 per cent of first-year students came from Paris and from wealthy families.

> Family is an important factor. We have a relatively large number of students whose father or mother went to the Polytechnique. Such candidates are motivated and believe in themselves. They think:' of course I can do it.' Things are different for a gifted student from, say, Strasbourg who is quickly inclined to think: 'Oh, the Polytechnique, that's not for the likes of me.[15]

The alumni of these institutions head up ministries, public enterprises and other large companies in which the state has a considerable influence. Around 60 per cent of the staff of President Hollande, himself an *énarque* (alumnus of ENA), went to either the polytechnique or the ENA. Xavier Broseta, the human resources manager at Air France set upon by his own staff, is another *énarque*. After graduating in 1995, he followed a typical career path. Having started at the Ministry of Labour, after seven years he transferred to the national healthcare system; in 2002, he went to work for national electronics giant Thales, followed by a position on the board of Air France. A career like that is like a warm bath; the alumni of the *grandes écoles* look after their own.

---

14 Suleiman (1974), p. 32.
15 *De Volkskrant*, 27 August 2015.

Could the strong emotions of the Air France staff on that October day be explained by the overwhelming sense of impotence towards those who debate and decide their fate? Will this system of a medium-sized country governed by a small, self-sustaining elite ever change? Or will the equally deep-rooted feelings of former President Pompidou, himself educated at the École Normale Supérieure (a *normalien*), continue to prevail: 'You are a *normalien*, in the same way you are of princely blood. You can't see it on the outside but you can feel it and you know it.'[16] This social division is not a recent development. Georges Simenon, creator of the famous Inspector Maigret, describes a provincial town in the 1950s after a murder has taken place in the street.

> The thing that struck Maigret was quite hard to define. The smaller of the two groups, the one closest to the body, seemed to be made up only of people who knew each other and belonged to a particular milieu: the magistrate, the two doctors, probably the men who had been playing bridge earlier with Doctor Jussieux and were doubtless all local bigwigs. The other, less illustrious group did not maintain the same silence. Without overtly showing it, they exuded a certain hostility. There were even a few sniggers.

Maigret happens to be in the town because he is visiting an old friend who is the local magistrate. A short while later when he takes the statement of a local school teacher that is incriminating to one of his posh friends, a full-blown class war erupts. ' "Do you stand by your statement?" "Yes, even if you don't like it." "This isn't about me." "It's about your friends." '[17]

The explanation for the strained labour relations could lie in the existence of an elite that looks after its own and only allows minimal access to newcomers. Giving in easily to open protest is a way of preventing such actions from inspiring other groups and evolving into mass movements. The unions are aware of this fear among the elite

---

16 *De Volkskrant*, 27 August 2015.
17 Simenon (2017), pp. 30, 70.

and therefore find it relatively easy to achieve their objectives, which revolve around retaining existing privileges. But this does nothing to lessen the underlying gap that separates the two parties.

Labour Relations in Sweden

Paper group SCA successfully transformed itself into a group making high-added-value paper-related products such as nappies, sanitary pads and toilet rolls. According to official statements, environmental targets were observed at all times during the transformation, and the company has 'zero tolerance for all forms of corrupt and unethical business practices'.

So it was no surprise why Swedish daily *Svenska Dagbladet* devoted an article in November 2014 to the group's practice of operating private jets with only one or two passengers on board. The journalists started digging and soon discovered that both executives and supervisory board members regularly availed themselves of this mode of transport to attend sporting events such as the Olympic Games in London, the European Football Championships in Kiev, Formula 1 car races and to visit luxury hunting cabins in northern Sweden (with the hunting dogs being ferried in by helicopter). Sometimes they were accompanied by PwC auditors, wives, children and pets. For example, CEO Jan Johansson travelled with his daughter to the World Cup in Brazil and became embroiled in a debate with the press as to whether his wife had accompanied him on 12 or 22 occasions.

Just one month after these revelations the company changed its travel policy to exclude family members. But the move had come too late: the whole country was in uproar at this flagrant abuse. Carl Rosén, managing director of the Swedish Shareholder Association which represents 60,000 small investors, described what happened next.

The first suggestion to let the auditors audit the travel policy was strongly opposed by the organisation I represent, the Swedish Shareholder Association. Together with institutional owners, we forced the board to hire truly independent investigators [...]. The unions, normally known to be very cooperative towards management, demanded resignation of the chair of SCA, Sverker Martin-Löf. The day after, he said that he would also leave all his six board seats in listed companies. Later on, the managing director of SCA, Jan Johansson, and his deputy were fired.[18]

On 31 January 2015, a few days after losing his job, Johansson was interviewed by a journalist from *Svenska Dagbladet*. The day before, it had been announced that the public prosecutor of the national anti-corruption unit was launching an investigation. Johansson's successor promptly hired over 500 auditors to check the accounts. Johansson was contrite in responding to the journalist's questions.

> I received an email from an employee at one of the SCA plants saying that they had been told to write their names on dispos-able plastic cups in order to save money. How do you think they feel when they read about you taking company planes to the World Cup and going on expensive hunting trips?' '... obvi-ously they are going to react, it would be weird if they didn't. I would do the same in that situation [...] I would think: what are they playing at?[19]

The wave of public outrage was not yet over. *Svenska Dagbladet* organised a seminar with the provocative title, 'Where does God stand on the private use of corporate jets?' To the annoyance of former chairman Martin-Löf, Archbishop of Sweden Antje Jackelén also waded into the debate. Plus the universally venerated author Henning Mankell described the conduct of the SCA executives and everyone else involved as 'typical of the greed and arrogance of the economic elite'.[20] Not wanting to be left out, Sweden's accountancy association said in a statement: 'It is very inappropriate that the auditor participates in an elk hunt that the client company organises and hosts.'[21]

A few months later, when the dust from the affair had settled, more than 10 management and board seats had been replaced at

18 Ethicalboardroom.com, 6 May 2015.
19 *Svenska Dagbladet*, 31 January 2015.
20 *Het Financieele Dagblad*, 28 April 2015.
21 *The Guardian*, 11 February 2015.

some of the country's biggest companies. SCA was not alone in being hit, with companies including Handelsbanken, SSAB, Sandvik and Industrivärden – all with close ties to SCA – also being affected. All had appointed new managers, mostly outsiders, and public apologies had been made. This had largely restored the public confidence in the entrepreneurial class, paving the way for the trade unions to resume the tradition of peaceful labour relations and close consultation with the employers.

The impact of Henning Mankell's criticism of certain executives' irresponsible wanderlust was all the greater because the entire country knew that the author only had months to live. Like many other detective writers, Mankell practiced a wide range of literary genres but mainly became known and loved for his stories featuring Ystad police inspector Kurt Wallander. In *The Troubled Man*, Wallander's daughter Linda has found true love and tells her father about how she first met her fiancé, a gentleman of standing, named Hans von Enke. Hans had been 'working for a finance company that specialised in setting up hedge funds. Linda had found him somewhat self-important, and had been annoyed by him. She informed him, rather fiercely, that she was a simple police officer, badly paid, and had no idea what a hedge fund was.' When Wallander is introduced to his future son-in-law two days later, his reaction is the same. 'Wallander immediately felt uncomfortable in his presence, found his way of expressing himself off-putting, and wondered what on earth had inspired Linda to take a shine to him.' This changes when Hans von Enke invites the inspector to his office and shows him around. 'Afterwards Hans invited him to lunch, and when Wallander returned to Ystad, he no longer had the feeling of inferiority that had affected him at their first meeting.' The pattern is repeated when Linda organises a dinner to which her future parents-in-law are also invited.

'I'm not used to mixing with the nobility,' said Wallander irritably when Linda finished speaking. 'They're just like everybody else. I think you'll find you have plenty to talk about.' This hunch turns out to be right. 'As Wallander sat in a taxi on the way back to Löderup at around midnight, he decided that the evening had turned out to be much more pleasant than he had expected.' The feeling is mutual, as Linda tells her father the next day. '[Hans' father] had a funny way of putting it. He said: 'Your dad is an excellent acquisition for the family.'[22]

Social class difference exists in Sweden, too. As ordinary middle-class people, at first the Wallanders look up to the posh Von Enkes. But the chill in the air is quickly dispelled and both father and daughter are able to appreciate the contact. On their part, the Von Enkes have no problem at all accepting a girl from a lower social class for their only son. On the contrary, they are genuinely pleased with the Wallander family.

Limited differences make for easier contact between members of different social classes. This is true both privately and in the public domain, where representatives of employers and employees cross paths. In the wake of the SCA corporate jet scandal, neither party wanted to put the advantages of their cooperation at risk. Once the guilty parties had been punished, the incident was put away with the collection of other scandals. Mutual trust had received a blow but had not suffered irreparable damage.

Conclusion

Social distinctions occur in every society. People set themselves apart from others by means of the neighbourhood they live in, how they spend their holidays, the restaurants they eat in, the clothes they wear and, last but not least, the way they interact. In France these distinctions are further emphasised by the existence of the *grandes écoles*. With these educational institutions only being accessible to a small group and providing the springboard for life-long careers, there is a social division that does not exist to the same extent in Sweden. This difference was apparent in the contact between a school master and the local magistrate in a small French town and the Wallanders and their future in-laws. When a scandal occurs, the way in which it is resolved also prompts different feelings among the elite and the general population, and this carries through into political and economic life. Can top executives and entrepreneurs be obliged to follow the rules that should apply to everyone? If the answer is yes, the trust

---

22 Mankell (2011), pp. 36–42.

between employers and employees will quickly be restored after a crisis. If the answer is no, structurally fractious labour relations will be the price that has to be paid.

Willingness to Delegate Authority

Delegating in Greece

After being appointed Prime Minister of Greece in October 2009, George Papandreou was keen to use the opportunity to realise his dream of a streamlined, digitised e-government (Table 2.3). One of his first actions was to set up an open internet platform for the selection of senior government officials: no more family members or cronies, but instead honest, transparent selection of the most qualified candidates. In November one such high-flyer, Diomedes Spinellis, professor of software engineering at Athens University of Economics and Business, was appointed head of the General Secretariat of Information Systems (GSIS) at the Ministry of Finance. Having used the open recruitment platform to attract five other whizz-kids, he set to work.

Tax collection was an obvious area in which to prove their skills because it was one where the government was missing out on a lot

Table 2.3 Willingness to delegate authority (1 = low, 10 = high)

Sweden	8.86
Denmark	8.57
Norway	8.29
The Netherlands	8.15
Germany	7.44
United Kingdom	7.15
Austria	7.01
Ireland	7.01
Average	*6.83*
France	5.86
Spain	5.58
Portugal	5.29
Greece	4.86
Italy	4.72

Source: World Economic Forum; average scores from the Global Competitiveness Reports, 2006–15 (inclusive).

of revenue. By linking various files, Spinellis and his team were able to compare taxpayers' declared income with the lifestyle they were leading. How could a successful medical specialist live in a luxury villa with a swimming pool and drive a BMW 5 Series on an annual salary of just 10,000 euros? The names involved in such cases were handed over to the 300 or so tax offices across the country, along with the request that the regional inspectorates investigate further and impose retrospective levies. To Spinellis's astonishment and disappointment not a single office took action in response to his material.

Next, the whizz-kids sought to boost government revenue by tackling fraud in the fuel trade. On 26 August 2011, Spinellis supplied Yannis Kapeleris, the Secretary General for Tax and Customs Affairs, with the names of 3,500 oil traders who had failed to enter their transactions in the official computer system in the first four months of the year in a bid to avoid being taxed. One might expect that Kapeleris, who had been working for the Finance Ministry for around 25 years, would be pleased to be provided with this information. Just a few months previously he had said in an interview: 'Greece is a poor state with rich people. For too long, the authorities have let evaders get away with it. Now we're going to be merciless and we're going to start with the big fish.'[23]

However, Kapeleris did not react as expected; he issued a guideline which determined that the imposition of fines on the fuel traders would be postponed until new legislation had come into force, thus undermining the entire operation. Spinellis had had enough and a few weeks later resigned 'for personal reasons'. In an interview with a research journalist he was more forthright: 'I would have been much happier at my post in the autumn of 2011 if there was a Secretary General of Tax and Customs Affairs who would call me day and night asking for data and offering ideas about how to combat tax evasion. It is well documented that this was not the case.'[24]

---

23 *The Guardian*, 20 October 2010. At the time of this interview Kapeleris was still head of the financial crimes unit. I have assumed that he did not change his views when he took over as secretary general for tax and customs affairs in April 2011.

24 Palaiologos (2014), p. 40.

Deputy Finance Minister Pantelis Economou was no more enthu-
siastic about Spinellis's work. 'It's correct he was generating reports
every afternoon', Mr. Economou said. 'These reports came to my
office [...] but there's no system to manage this phenomenon.'[25]

How was it possible that the minister, who during the period in
question was responsible for negotiating with the troika[26] about new
foreign loans, chose to side with Kapeleris and the tax inspectors?
And how was it possible that the minister chose to let down those
who were in a position to give government revenue a boost in the
short term? Where was this unwillingness coming from? Professor of
Public Finance Nikos Tatsos, who had been involved in attempts to
improve government functioning for over 30 years, knew the answer.

'You cannot go in there (the Finance Ministry – ed.) using a regular
army', he said. 'You've got sharp-shooters shooting at you left and
right. It's a guerrilla war and you need to use irregular methods to
succeed.'

It was clear that Papandreou's whizz-kids were not made of the
right stuff to win this war, something lamented by Professor Tatsos.

These fine minds are wasted in a place where there is no strategic thinking, where no one sees the bigger picture and fresh
minds are not allowed to contribute meaningfully until they
reach a certain level in the hierarchy, which takes twenty years.
By that time they have lost the ability to think, to process data.
Young people get buried in the system.[27]

Spinellis had sinned against the system. As a newcomer, he had
not carried out the instructions of long-serving senior civil servants
but had instead reversed the process, sending lists of names of tax
evaders to powerful officials along with a request to deal with them.

---

25 *New York Times*, 2 February 2012.
26 The troika is a term used to designate the International Monetary Fund, the
    European Central Bank and the European Commission, which together were
    responsible for the change programmes which Greece had to implement in
    order to obtain the massive loans it needed in order to remain a member of
    the Eurozone.
27 Palaiologos (2014), pp. 33, 44.

After which he had the temerity to check up on them and kick up a fuss when they failed to take action. With their dignity in tatters, the old guard in the end had to put up with Spinellis for two years. It is likely they breathed a sigh of relief when he left, favouring lower revenue for the government coffers over adopting a new approach. Or in the words of Professor Tatsos, 'The old guard viewed the GSIS team (the Spinellis team – ed.) and their innovations the way the Indians used to view the train.'[28]

Is this unwillingness to delegate power and influence to younger, sometimes more junior, members of staff exclusive to the Finance Ministry or is it also prevalent at other institutions? The adventures of Inspector Costas Haritos give us an insight into how things work within the Greek police force. In the detective story *The Late-night News* the inspector is thinking about how to deal with his assistant Thanassis.

> The chief wanted to see me. To ask how was the case going. And Thanassis hadn't brought me my breakfast because he was certain that once I heard that the Chief wanted to see me, I'd drop everything and rush upstairs. 'Your job is to bring me my coffee and croissant. I'll decide when I see the Chief,' I told him angrily and leaned back into my chair to show him that I had no intention of budging from my desk all morning. The smile immediately vanished from his face. All his assuredness went out of the window. 'Yes, sir,' he mumbled. 'Well – what are you waiting for?' He turned on his heel and sprang out of the office. I waited a minute or two and then got up to go and see the Chief. I wouldn't have put it past Thanassis to let it be known that the Chief wanted to see me and that I was playing the smart alec. And the Chief knew every trick in the book; you had to watch your back with him.[29]

The scene shows us three layers of the police hierarchy. Inspector Haritos represents the middle layer: ranked above his assistant

---

28 Palaiologos (2014), p. 42.
29 Markaris (2005), p. 12.

Thanassis but below Superintendent Ghikas. Thanassis keeps a close eye on how his immediate superior responds to orders from the superintendent. Haritos is aware of this; there is a chance that his assistant will tell if he fails to respond adequately. On the other hand, Haritos wants to appear important to his assistant, someone who will not be bossed around. In short, no one at the police station trusts each other. What are things like further up in the hierarchy?

Haritos has been charged with investigating the murder of two journalists working for a TV station. The station's director, Delopoulos, has the power to make or break the minister. Charitos's boss, Superintendent Ghikas, sides with the hierarchy. 'The Minister and Delopoulos were side by side on the sofa, as if wishing to make it clear to me that they were close friends. Ghikas was sitting in the armchair next to the Minister [...] The scene spoke for itself. Delopoulos wanted my head on a plate, the Minister wanted to humour him in order to keep in with him. And as for Ghikas, he had his own ambitions.' Television director Delopoulos wants the case out of the public eye as soon as possible and for the blame to fall on an outsider, X. But Inspector Haritos refuses to play ball. ' "I would be astonished if X turned out to be a psychopathic killer, Minister.' And I gave him the whole spiel about psychopaths [...] 'I'm sure Superintendent Ghikas must have told you all this,' I added. Ghikas knew all that, but I was certain he hadn't said anything to them, because it was in his interests to follow their tack.'[30]

Ghikas and the minister have charged the inspector with finding the killer but this scene makes it clear that he does not have their support. On the contrary, they want him to do as the media magnate wishes and make an arrest as soon as possible. The mutual distrust and office politics that we encountered earlier among the lower ranks at the police station are mirrored here; nobody trusts anybody. Delegating does occur, simply because there is no other option, but is not based on trust. In the same way as happened to the real-life Spinellis of the Finance Ministry, if a scapegoat is needed, the fictional Inspector Haritos will be sacrificed.

---

30 Ibid., p. 185.

Delegating in the Netherlands

With over 12 years in office, Gerrit Zalm was the longest-serving finance minister in Dutch history. After resigning, rather than resting on his laurels, he took on the responsibility of heading up ABN Amro, one of the largest Dutch banks. After taking over as CEO in 2009, Zalm started writing a daily blog to give employees 'an impression of what I'm up to and what is occupying my thoughts'. On 21 July 2011, he shared his views on his own role. 'Regularly attend meetings [...], where I am not a voting member. Consider myself to be a participant rather than "the boss." Underestimate the impact, because others do see me as "the boss." Both sides need to learn here. I need to try and hold my tongue for longer and the others need to learn to disagree with "the boss."' Just under a year later it would appear that this objective has been achieved. Zalm's blog describes a meeting on 4 June 2012.

> With X, I discussed the main areas of concern at Risk Management. Took advantage of the opportunity to compliment him on his chairmanship of the Central Credit Committee. He had studied all the cases in detail, gave all those present the space to voice their opinion, before drawing clear conclusions. I was also very pleased with how he dealt with my presence. I am an 'outside member' who turns up once in a while and am granted no special privileges. Looked over at me last – to see if I wanted to add anything – and I think that's quite something.

Sometimes Zalm would address the bank as a whole, to urge staff to behave in the manner he would like.

> Do whatever you can, hold colleagues and managers to account, walk up the down escalator. Do not take no for an answer and pursue the yes. That's how we will create the bank that we want [...] I have heard many of the critical remarks before [...] Challenge yourself, your colleagues and your manager. Why can't we do that? Who says so? And have you called them out

on that? And if you don't get the right answer, have you tried taking it higher up? (21 June 2011)[31]

Zalm's blog devotes hardly any space to mistakes made by employees. In his memoir *The Romantic Bookkeeper* he opens up a bit more about his time as finance minister. For example, he tells of the time he organised a festive gathering at Wittenburg castle in Wassenaar for his former German counterpart Theo Waigel, who was to be presented with a high Dutch honour.

> The official invitation, which went out under my name, stated the dress code as 'black tie' and that means dinner jackets for the gentlemen. Everyone present had received an invitation except me. I was the only one to arrive in a business suit [...] The hosting minister as the only person in a normal suit: not good form. Fred van Asch van Wijck, my head of protocol, suggested that we swap suits; he did have on a dinner jacket. We retreated to a back room and exchanged clothes. With Fred being taller than me my new trousers were pooling a bit at the ankles, but it wasn't too noticeable.[32]

Delegating entails risks. In this case, the oversight was that of the head of the protocol department but Zalm did not seem to mind. He accepted the proffered solution and put up with his bizarre outfit without reproaching Fred van Asch van Wijck.

To see whether Gerrit Zalm is the only one in Holland who does not take the official hierarchy too seriously, let us compare his actions to those of the fictitious Inspector DeKok of Warmoesstraat police station in Amsterdam. The story *DeKok and the Dying Stroller* revolves around a poisoning case. DeKok's younger colleague Vledder wants to handle the case himself but the experienced detective has his doubts.

---

31 In his blog of 21 July 2011, Gerrit Zalm granted me permission to quote from his work. I thank him for his trust.
32 Zalm (2009), p. 360.

Just one look at Vledder's face told him all he needed to know
[...] 'So you think,' he said resignedly, 'that you can handle this
case?' Vledder nodded vaguely. 'Yes [...] I think so.' DeKok
rubbed the bridge of his nose with a little finger. It took several
seconds [...] then he had reached a conclusion. 'Alright,' he
said tersely, 'then you should.'

Chief Superintendent Buitendam, the boss of both detectives, is
dead set against the decision. 'This case is too serious [...] too deli-
cate. I simply cannot afford to leave it in the hands of a young, inexperienced officer.' But DeKok refuses to budge. 'The chief of police
rubbed a thin hand over his pale face. He knew that an unwilling
DeKok was completely unmanageable. 'I get it,' he said slowly. 'Any
discussion is pointless. There's no talking to you.' He nodded to himself. 'Alright [...] I will give Vledder the order to take over the case
from you. It might be for the best.'[33]

It would appear that the Dutch superiors are not only prepared
to give younger members of staff their own responsibility at a fairly
early stage but that those members of staff actually request it. If they
are not given that trust, it causes tensions. The younger employees
are able to take that risk because they know that any failures will not
be held against them too badly. At the same time delegating a lot
of duties has the advantage of enabling superiors to deal with more
cases than if they had to handle everything themselves.

Conclusion

The differences between the Netherlands and Greece are huge. It
takes around 20 years for a civil servant at the Greek Finance Ministry
to get any say. By contrast, at the age of 26 and after just three years
at the ministry, Gerrit Zalm was appointed Head of the budget preparation department.

The same can be seen in the detective stories. Both the Greek and
the Dutch story cited describe the relations between three successive
levels of the police hierarchy. While the junior detective in Greece is
expected to fetch coffee for his boss, his Dutch counterpart succeeds

---

33 Baantjer (1994), pp. 34–36.

in being made responsible for a murder case. These enormous fictional and real-life differences are reflected in the very different scores in the table showing the willingness to delegate authority.

Is the Judiciary Independent?

The Judiciary in the United Kingdom

The phone-hacking scandal involving tabloid newspaper *News of the World* (NoW) was not just about the illegal hacking of people's voicemail and mobile phones but also about bribery and intimidation of police officials and other people with information of interest to the newspaper – generally the sex lives of celebrities (Table 2.4). The affair came to a head on 4 July 2014 when the highest criminal court in the land, the Old Bailey, presented its verdict after a trial which lasted eight months and enthralled the nation.

Mr Justice Saunders commenced his sentencing with an explanation of his own role. 'Parliament has decided that it is a criminal offence to access the voicemails of other people without their consent or an order of the court. Parliament has decided that the offence

Table 2.4 Is the judiciary independent? (1 = no, 10 = completely independent)

Denmark	9.15
The Netherlands	9.01
Sweden	9.01
Germany	9.01
Ireland	9.01
Norway	8.87
United Kingdom	8.72
Austria	8.15
Average	*7.76*
France	7.15
Portugal	6.72
Spain	5.58
Greece	5.29
Italy	5.15

Source: World Economic Forum; average scores from the Global Competitiveness Reports, 2006–15 (inclusive).

applies to members of the press in the same way as it does to all other citizens [...] My function is to pass sentences which reflect the criminality of the defendants as defined by that law [...] It is not my job to pass judgment on, or make observations about, the relationship between the press, the police and the politicians [...] What is an important matter for me to have in mind in considering sentence is the amount of phone hacking that went on for the benefit of the News of the World and over what period. It had started by April 2002 when Milly Dowler's phone was hacked.'[34]

Milly Dowler was a 13-year-old schoolgirl who was abducted on her way home from school. Her body was found six months later. In his sentence the judge explained how the tragedy was connected to NoW.

Andy Coulson was editing the paper in the absence of Rebekah Brooks. Glenn Mulcaire, a private investigator hired by NoW, picked up a message left on Milly Dowler's phone by an employment agency in Telford [...] We now know that the message was left by mistake on Milly's phone and was intended for someone who had a similar mobile phone number and name [...] The News of the World didn't know that, and a team of reporters were despatched to find her. They failed. As we now know, Milly was already dead. The News of the World delayed telling the police the contents of the voicemail until they realised that they were not going to find Milly. That was unforgiveable [...] Their true motivation was not to act in the best interests of the child but to get credit for finding her and thereby sell the maximum number of newspapers.

With her long red curls Rebekah Brooks is arguably the best-known journalist in the United Kingdom. She started work at NoW as a secretary in 1989 at the age of 20 and some 10 years later became the youngest editor of a British national newspaper. By coincidence she was holidaying in Dubai at the time of the tragedy and could therefore not be held responsible. That does not change the fact that the

34 Judiciary of England and Wales: R –v– Coulson and others, Central Criminal Court, 4 July 2014.

phones of thousands of celebrities and ordinary people were hacked and tapped during her time as editor. In this way NoW and *The Sun*, which was part of the same group and where Brooks served as deputy editor (from 1998 to 2000), managed to obtain sensitive information to boost their newsstand sales. In 2000, Brooks gained access to confidential medical information concerning Fraser Brown, son of the later Prime Minister Gordon Brown. She wasted no time in phoning the politician to inform him that *The Sun* was set to reveal that his son had cystic fibrosis and sought to persuade him not to announce the news himself but to give the scoop to the newspaper. While this type of story makes Brooks look like an insensitive bully, it does not mean that any hard evidence was obtained in this way that could provide grounds for her conviction. Of the more than 11,000 pages of notes kept by the hackers seized by the police, only 12 hacked voicemail messages could be linked to the period when she was editor. Moreover, Brooks was not mentioned by name in any of these messages. In light of this the judge had no choice but to acquit her.

For Andy Coulson, Brooks' deputy who succeeded her as editor of NoW (in 2003), things were different. Justice Saunders showed him no mercy.

> Mr Coulson, on the jury's verdict, has to take the major share of the blame for the phone hacking at the News of the World. There is insufficient evidence to conclude that he started the phone hacking but there is ample evidence that it increased enormously while he was the editor. On the jury's verdict he knew about it and encouraged it when he should have stopped it.[35]

Andy Coulson was sentenced to jail along with three other journalists. Given that Coulson had in the meantime been appointed director of communication to Prime Minister David Cameron, the sentence was also damaging to the most powerful politician of the United Kingdom. Cameron was contrite. 'I am extremely sorry I employed him. It was the wrong decision.' Asked what checks he had made before employing Coulson, Cameron said: 'I asked him questions, if

---

35 www.bbc.co.uk/news/uk-politics-27998411, 24 June 2014.

he knew about phone hacking, and he said he didn't and I accepted those assurances and I gave him the job.'[36]

Journalist Nick Davies played a major part in exposing NoW, relentlessly pursuing not just the newspaper but the entire multinational media group of billionaire Rupert Murdoch from 2008. He describes his battle, which reads like an exciting detective story, in his book *Hack Attack*. What is his verdict on the trial and the functioning of the judiciary? Davies points out that the outcome of the trial was not a foregone conclusion. Aside from the fact that the public prosecution had considerably fewer resources at its disposal than the defence lawyers acting on behalf of the Murdoch empire, he believes there was a lack of hard evidence. He therefore accepts Rebekah Brooks' acquittal and concludes: 'The trial was a fair result.'[37]

It is likely that Davies is also pleased about the many follow-up investigations which have taken place. Countless journalists, private detectives, police officers and other officials have been questioned since then. Some have been taken to court and sentenced. Given the scope of the scandal, which also involved other tabloids besides NoW and *The Sun*, it would seem that this is the maximum result that can be achieved.

The best-known fictional legal sleuth in the United Kingdom is Horace Rumpole. For many years the public lapped up the criminal lawyer's adventures on television, radio and in books. In *Rumpole and the Golden Thread* the hero is invited by one of his former students to defend him in his faraway country. In prison the young man recites the old lessons.

'A man is innocent until he's proved guilty. Better that ten guilty men should go free than one who is not guilty should be convicted, for to convict the innocent is [...]' The words sounded particularly convincing in his dark velvet voice, and I joined in the chorus, 'To spit in the face of justice.'[38]

---

36 Ibid.
37 Davies (2015), p. 401.
38 Mortimer (1983), p. 71.

Back in England, a judge in another trial gives the members of the jury some good advice before they present their verdict. 'If you are certain that, for whatever reason, Mrs X deliberately shot her husband with the intention of killing or seriously wounding him, then you must convict her. But if you believe that the account that she has given you could be true – I say could be – then she deserves to be acquitted […] This Court does not make value judgements […] What we are concerned with is certainty and the truth.'[39]

This view is echoed in the verdict given by the real-life Justice Saunders: as there is no irrefutable evidence that Rebekah Brooks gave instructions for people's phones to be tapped she must be acquitted. The same does not apply to Andy Coulson. In addition we must conclude that the judge was able to do his work without interference from powerful politicians such as David Cameron or billionaire moguls such as Rupert Murdoch. The UK judiciary enjoys a high degree of independence, not just in theory but in practice, too.

The Judiciary in Italy

On 17 February 1992, judge Antonio di Pietro ordered the arrest of Socialist politician Mario Chiesa for accepting a bribe from a Milan cleaning firm. The leader of the Italian Socialist Party (PSI) Bettino Craxi immediately distanced himself from the suspect, calling Chiesa a 'marioulo', or 'villain', a 'wild splinter' of his otherwise squeaky-clean party. Angry at this response, Chiesa supplied the judge with information about countless other corruption scandals. This marked the beginning of the *Mani Pulite* ('clean hands') operation, the biggest legal investigation into political corruption since the Second World War. Two years later, all four political parties in government in 1992 had disappeared, including the dominant Christian Democracy (DC). This episode, instigated and implemented by the judiciary, is called the end of the First Republic.

The process was watched with interest by the successful Milanese businessman Silvio Berlusconi, who set up a new centre-right political party, Forza Italia, to fill the vacuum left by the collapse of the Christian Democrats. After winning the election, he took office as

---

39 Ibid., pp. 212–13.

prime minister in the spring of 1994. However, this did not end the battle between the judiciary and the politicians. On the contrary, Justice Di Pietro ordered an investigation into Berlusconi's companies, to which the new government responded by sending inspectors into the Public Prosecutor's Office – to search for irregularities. There was no winner in this first round; in December 1994 both Di Pietro and Berlusconi stepped down.

Berlusconi, however, proved to be more than a political flash in the pan. Under the slogan 'I want a revolution' he and his coalition partner Lega Nord won a parliamentary majority in the 2001 elections and Berlusconi was appointed prime minister for the second time. One aspect of this 'revolution' was legislation that made a large section of the population wonder whether it was designed to benefit the country or to protect Berlusconi's private interests. For example, the law on false accounting was changed so that public prosecutors were no longer allowed to initiate investigations into the accounts of companies they suspected of fraud. From then on it would be up to the injured party to take the legal initiative and prove that they have suffered financial damage. It is unclear whether, as the government expects, the small- and medium-sized business sector benefited from this change in the law. What is clear is that Berlusconi himself did, as is evidenced by the case against his Fininvest media group, which was accused of illegally siphoning off 750 million euros to 64 offshore companies. With no injured party coming forward, the case lapsed.

The new government also changed the immunity law, improving Berlusconi's ability to defend himself against a charge of bribing judges when a rival looked set to snap up state-owned food group SME from under his nose. The transaction was blocked by Rome judge Renato Squillante in 1985. Later it emerged that an intermediary had paid the judge 434,000 dollars out of a Swiss bank account held by Berlusconi for private purposes. The Public Prosecutor smelt blood and sought the maximum sentence of eight years in jail. She said that for years Berlusconi had had several judges on his payroll 'and as prime minister he came into this courtroom to lie'.[40]

It was to no avail, given that Parliament had since adopted the Lodo Maccanico act, guaranteeing immunity from prosecution to

---

40 *The Telegraph*, 11 December 2004.

those holding the five highest offices of the state. Naturally, as Prime Minister Berlusconi was one of these.[41]

In this way Berlusconi managed to outwit the magistrates in dozens of cases. However, in 2013, by which time Berlusconi was no longer prime minister, they finally managed to get him in the Mediaset trial. Mediaset was a Berlusconi company that was accused in 2005 of illegally trading film rights with fictitious companies in overseas tax havens. These transactions resulted in losses for Mediaset in Italy while the profits accumulated abroad; these were then channelled back to Italy as personal income without any income tax being paid on them. The prosecutor accused Berlusconi of having cheated the tax authorities out of 7.3 million euros in this way. In 2012, a court sentenced the former prime minister to four years in jail and banned him from holding public office for five years. A year later the verdict was upheld on appeal, with a few amendments. The highest court, the Court of Cassation, fast-tracked the case to prevent it from lapsing. On that day comedian/politician Beppe Grillo wrote in his blog: 'His conviction is like the fall of the Berlin Wall in 1989.' Given that Berlusconi was still a member of the Senate at that point and senators had by then also been granted immunity, this body still had to decide whether to lift immunity in his case. On 27 November 2013, Berlusconi was expelled from the Senate and for the first time had to serve his sentence. The prison sentence was converted into a term of community service, but he was still banned from seeking public office. This largely settled the duel between Berlusconi and the judiciary. As was the case during the period of the First Republic there is no doubt that politicians and the judiciary still exert a strong mutual influence. Journalist Giuliano Ferrara summed it up as follows. 'There is no point in blaming him for thinking about his own business and for wanting to protect himself against eager magistrates and his wealth against verdicts that on paper would seek to chop it into pieces [...] Mr Berlusconi's business is the business of the nation. End of story.'[42]

---

41 Subsequently, various drafts of the act were rejected by the Constitutional Court. Despite this, Berlusconi was definitively acquitted of the charges in April 2007.
42 Quoted in Severgnini (2011), p. 43.

Of course, the question remains as to whether Berlusconi is an exception in this respect or whether we must accept that the judicial, political and economic powers in Italy form a single inextricable tangle in which they intertwine, influence and sustain one another in countless ways.

When it is announced that despite his advanced age the 90-year-old author Andrea Camilleri has come up with a new adventure for his Inspector Salvo Montalbano, the whole of Italy rejoices. Ever since the first film adaptation (in 1999) the Sicilian hero has been a real ratings winner. It would seem that the author touches a sensitive national chord. In these crime stories all kinds of powerful people get themselves into trouble after which their accomplices, who often work in the public sector, are engaged to stage a cover-up. In *Excursion to Tindari* Montalbano tracks down traffickers in human organs for transplantation into important people who are in need of them. 'If this ever came out, they'd be finished, whatever their position, whether at the top of a government, economic empire or banking conglomerate.'

Montalbano fears that the official authorities will take no action against these people in power and therefore passes the information on to a journalist friend who breaks the story on television. This scuppers any chance of the case being hushed up. 'They all came running, the police commissioner, the chief public prosecutor [...]'[43] Only under pressure of public opinion are the authorities prepared to take steps. No wonder people don't trust them.

In another story the judge asks Montalbano to pay 'an informal visit' to the lawyer of an important person. 'And respectful. In short, we need to put on the kid gloves.' The inspector understands the reason for this instruction to proceed with caution when he examines the photographs that the lawyer has, not by chance, displayed in his waiting room. 'They were all of politicians: senators, deputies of the chamber, ministers, former or current undersecretaries. All signed and dedicated to the "dear" or "dearest" Mr Luna.'[44]

---

43 Camilleri (2005), pp. 279, 285.
44 Ibid., pp. 204–6.

The weak position of the judiciary in this force field is illustrated in *The fear of Montalbano* by the open criticism expressed by a politician in a television interview.

> There were people, decent people of impeccable character – said his excellency the undersecretary in a voice shaking with indignation – who had always fought for justice, who had even assumed the function of the state when it proved lacking, and the so-called judiciary had rewarded them by branding them as mafiosi! This would never happen again under this new government, concluded his excellency to rapturous applause.[45]

In so doing, politicians undermine the position of the judiciary. They permit the law to be upheld by private parties and not just by institutions of the state. The fact that such parties tend to have their own agendas is not seen as a problem. The fictitious undersecretary reminds us of the real-life Berlusconi who, despite holding high office, expresses his aversion to the judiciary in many different ways. 'This is a manifest judicial persecution, which I am proud to resist, and the fact that my resistance and sacrifice will give the Italians a more fair and efficient judicial system makes me even more proud.'[46]

Camilleri's fiction is not just plucked out of thin air but turns out to be based on the reality of his home country. What a difference with the United Kingdom, where Justice Saunders does not hesitate to obstruct the most powerful politicians and businesspeople without having to fear their revenge. Barrister Rumpole also operates in the name of the law. Even in the world of British fantasy, powerful offenders who can do as they please without being punished strike us as implausible.

Conclusion

We have compared the way in which people work together in various institutions in 13 Western European countries. Whether we are looking

---

45 Ibid., pp. 119–20.
46 http://news.bbc.co.uk/1/hi/world/europe/4007441.stm, 12 November 2004.

at the way the civil service operates, the relations between employers and employees, delegating in the workplace or the functioning of the judiciary, in each case there turns out to be a north/south divide. In the case of the 'hard' figures of the World Economic Forum it makes no difference whether we take the average scores (over a 10-year period) or the most recent calendar year: the northern countries score higher than the average for the 13 countries, the southern countries score lower.

Is this distinction significant to the European integration process? Are all those government leaders and their advisers right when they assume (implicitly) that such differences are irrelevant when they make new agreements about adding another brick to the EU structure? Or are the differences identified important after all and will there be a price to pay for this at some point? Before addressing these questions, in the next chapter I will look at how people in different European countries punish those who do not cooperate enough. Will this result in the same split or will we see completely different combinations of countries?

Chapter 3

COOPERATION AND PUNISHMENT

The Périgord is a beautiful region of southwestern France, largely consisting of a limestone plateau cut through by rivers such as the Dordogne and the Vézère. As well as deep gorges these rivers have carved many caves and deep ridges in the steep valley walls. Human habitation of this area dates back to before the peak of the last ice age around 20,000 years ago. These modern humans ('*Homo sapiens*') started migrating to new regions from their original habitat in East Africa around 100,000 years ago. In the Périgord they made homes on the rocky ledges along the river valleys. Nowadays they are mainly famous for the cave art discovered here, with beautiful pictures of mammoths, reindeer and other wild animals. Who were these people who were able to thrive in this rich region? Who were the most successful? Darwin would say they were those who were best equipped, the best hunters, the best trackers or the best fire makers, while the most successful women were likely to be those who were most fertile or best at finding roots.

It is likely that no single one of these skills was decisive given that our ancestors were only able to survive in groups. An individual, no matter how brilliant, would be unlikely to survive for more than a year in these surroundings. Anthropological research has shown that hunter-gatherers normally lived in groups of between 20 and 70 people.[1] Such groups obviously benefited from having a few superior hunters and root-gatherers, but the most important thing was their members' ability to work together. They had to be able to share out essential tasks, be attuned to one another and be prepared to share and help each other. That means that the best hunter had to

---

1 Liljegren (1993), p. 93.

be prepared to share his kill with other hunters as well as with the
women and children who stayed behind at the campfire. The survival
of the fittest applies at group level as well as individual level. The
tribe or clan that was best able to cooperate was able to defeat competing groups in the contest for hunting grounds and other sought-
after assets. No matter how strong or clever, individual members of
tribes with inferior cooperation skills were destined to lose this battle.

Right up to the present day, the human species is the product of
this competition between groups and between individuals within
groups. This explains why we are capable of individual thought but
also devote a great deal of our energy to working with others. We,
along with the societies we form, are all characterised by combinations of these two selection criteria. We all have both self-seeking
and sociable characteristics. There are no extremes: completely
dominant group selection would lead to an ant-like population of
mutually indistinguishable individuals, while completely individual
selection would make all members of the group selfish and deceitful
and the group would fall apart.[2] Today, as well as in the past, human
groups differ from one another as a result of the relative importance
of group selection and individual selection. Is a society dominated by
self-serving free-riders or by people who work together and put the
interests of the group first?

What are these relations like in modern-day Western Europe? Let
us try to answer this question using game theory, a branch of math-
ematics in which strategic behaviour plays a key role. In the following
paragraphs I will discuss how cooperation works in various Western
European countries. Once again, my examples are taken from both
real-life news stories and crime novels.

Investing in a Joint Project

The Science of Games

As is the case with board games, a 'game' in this context refers to the
interaction between a number of players who together form a group
but take their own individual decisions. The success of each player

2 Wilson (2012), p. 243.

depends not just on their own choices but also on those made by the other players. How the members of a group influence each other's behaviour is one of the key topics studied by game theorists.

There are many different kinds of games. Given that we are interested in the integration process of various European countries we will concentrate on how members of a group interact with one another over several rounds of the game in order to realise joint projects. In our case the individual countries combined to form a European group, working together in many different areas, such as trade with non-European countries, environmental policy (no more plastic bags from 1 January 2016), the euro and the reception of refugees. As decisions on all such common projects require a large number of meetings (usually in Brussels), we are interested in how the decision-making process takes shape over the course of various rounds.

The 'public good game' chosen as an example here involves play by several teams, each composed of four students from a certain country. Each individual player receives 20 tokens, some or all of which they can invest in a joint project. The total combined investment amount is calculated for each group and a fixed reward is paid out at the end of each round. All members of the group receive the same amount, regardless of how much they put in. The four members of the group are not acquainted and decide the amount of their investment at the same time. Ten of these rounds are played in all. After each round the players are told how much each of the other members of the group invested. It goes without saying that this information will have a bearing on how much they invest in the next round.

There are two ways of playing this game: with or without the possibility to punish other members of the group by imposing a fine. As the table shows, the two variations of the game produce significantly different results (see Table 3.1). If the option with punishment is chosen, the table shows that the average investment by the eight countries over 10 rounds of the game rose from 7.3 to 11.4 tokens. It should be noted that this increase is mainly noticeable among the northern countries. The study shows that people from these countries mainly use the punishment option to push members of the group who invest relatively small amounts. These last generally understand

Table 3.1 Investment amount (from 0 to 20 tokens)

Average Investment	Without Punishment	With Punishment
Denmark	11.5	17.7
Switzerland (German-speaking)	9.7	16.5
Germany	9.2	14.5
United Kingdom	7.0	15.0
Average	*7.3*	*11.4*
France	5.0	9.6
Spain	6.1	7.3
Greece	6.4	5.7
Italy	3.5	4.5

Source: Hermann, Thöni and Gächter (2008 and 2010); Masclet and Villeval (for France, 2008); Casari and Luini (for Italy, 2009); Alonso (for Spain, 2013). These publications virtually replicate the 2002 study by Gächter and Fehr for these countries. I have been unable to find comparable research for the other countries.

the signal and make this clear by raising their investment in the next round. It transpires that for these countries 'social' punishment almost always results in higher investment in the joint project in each successive round. However, without this possibility of punishing free-riders, the other group members also become less motivated and will lower their investment in subsequent rounds.

In the four southern countries the average sum invested in both variations of the game is smaller than in the north. In Greece, the average investment is actually lower if the option of punishment is included. It transpires that some players from these countries fine other members of the group who invested more in the joint project than they themselves did in the previous round or rounds. This is a surprising result given that they benefit from the higher investments by their teammates in the form of the higher rewards paid out to all players at the end of each round. It would seem that motives other than financial ones are in play here. 'Antisocial' punishment would appear to be linked mainly to the leading position held by certain individuals in the group; the status of these individuals is undermined if other members of the group invest more than they do. By punishing team members for this type of behaviour the leaders are letting them know that such 'social' behaviour will not be appreciated in subsequent rounds.[3] The leaders of the groups accept that protecting their personal position could weaken both the joint project and the relative strength of their group compared to others.

Does this difference in behaviour between the north and the south of the continent only occur in games or also in other contexts? What can the detectives teach us about this? I will first look at cooperation and then move onto how different countries approach punishment.

Cooperation in the Netherlands and Italy

The Netherlands

During the hunt for the murderer of an Amsterdam judge, Inspector DeKok and his young sidekick Vledder stray off their own beat. They want to speak to the Public Prosecutor involved and find him in his home, poisoned.

> 'Shall we take it as evidence?' 'What?' 'The wine glass.' DeKok shook his head. 'We're not touching anything. We have no jurisdiction in Blaricum and I don't want competence issues getting us in trouble. Let's call in our colleagues from the Gooi- en Vechtstreek region and explain how we've wound up here [...] and why.' Vledder gave him a searching look. 'Are we also going to tell them all about our findings about the judge's murder?' DeKok nodded. 'Of course.'[4]

The scene is self-explanatory. Vledder wants to go after the murderer himself, but his boss, the experienced inspector, resists the temptation. That would only lead to trouble because of course the colleagues from the other region will eventually find out exactly what happened. It is much wiser to be honest with them and work together to achieve a result.

---

3 This subject has been widely researched, for example, by Nowak and Rand (2011).

4 Baantjer (1997), pp. 67–68.

Italy

How does DeKok's Italian counterpart act in a similar situation? At some point, Montalbano receives an anonymous letter claiming that a fatal accident at a building site was in fact murder. The event had taken place in a nearby village that comes under the jurisdiction of the colleagues of the carabinieri. Montalbano discusses the case with a colleague. 'We have two choices: we can either take the letter, burn it, and pretend we never received it, or muster all our courage – for we'll need all of it to do something like this – and send the letter to the carabinieri.' At that point, another colleague walks in and gives his views on the matter. 'We'll start by conducting a small investigation and we'll take it from there. If things go well, that is, if we turn up something concrete, we'll keep investigating [...] However, if we meet a dead end.' He stopped there and Montalbano finished his sentence: 'We'll send everything to the carabinieri and they can take it from there.'[5]

Cooperation Italian style is not at all the same as the Dutch variety. The game is more cunning and more ruthless. The impression that Montalbano and his immediate colleagues are more afraid of the carabinieri than the murderer is confirmed after the inspector has decided to carry on with the investigation himself: 'They had to proceed on the down low, without any rumors reaching the murderer, or worse the carabinieri.'[6]

Real-Life Events

What does cooperation in the real world look like in these two countries? Politics offers examples aplenty. Do you remember the spring of 2012? We were in the middle of the euro crisis and when the ruling coalition of Liberals and Christian Democrats in the Netherlands fell without warning, the consequences for the financial markets were plain to see. The yield on Dutch government bonds rose sharply and the stock market plummeted. What could be done?

---

5 Camilleri (2007), p. 125.
6 Ibid., p. 126.

The government crisis had been triggered by Geert Wilders who, on behalf of his party, suddenly withdrew his tacit support for the minority government when the time came to agree austerity measures. Without such measures the government deficit would exceed the limits set for euro countries, leaving the Netherlands vulnerable to financial speculators. Under these circumstances it took the government only a few days to reach an agreement with three other political parties on a new austerity package. The newspapers were jubilant.

> Courage. Hope. Self-sacrifice. Responsibility. Politicians used big words to describe what happened yesterday in the Lower House. And to a large extent these were justified.[7]

When the next general elections came around a few months later, it became clear that the electorate had not forgotten the crisis. Geert Wilders's march to success was rudely interrupted with his party seeing a 35 per cent drop in votes. The common interest, which is served by cooperation between various parties, was considered more important than the self-interest of an individual political party.

To gain an impression of how cooperation works in Italy let the United States go back to the early 1990s when the Milan judiciary brought down the corrupt First Republic. In addition to Antonio Di Pietro the *Pool di Mani Pulite* ('clean hands team') also comprised Gherardo Colombo. Some 25 years after the victory Colombo spoke of what had happened next.

> Many citizens distanced themselves from us. As long as the evidence was leading us to people in high places, everyone was happy. But our investigations also led us to the guy from the labour inspectorate who had accepted an envelope in return for not checking the safety precautions. And to the tax inspector who did not look too closely, the police officer who looked the other way. That's when people started asking: 'Are they going to check us out too?' Everyone was petrified.[8]

---

7 *NRC Handelsblad*, 27 April 2012.
8 *NRC Handelsblad*, 30 December 2015.

The people of Italy had been unable to break with the past and establish a political process in which the common good takes precedence over individual interests. By then it was clear that the Second Republic, with Silvio Berlusconi as its most prominent exponent, was not functioning much better than its predecessor. By 2007, Colombo had had enough. In the same interview he stated his conclusion as follows: 'There was no point any more. If you want to change things in my country, you won't get there by applying the law.' It would seem that cooperation in Italy is more difficult than in the Netherlands, not just in public good games and crime novels but also in the reality of everyday life. Both scientific games and fiction turn out to be suitable ways of analysing cooperation in different countries. Does the same apply to how people punish one another?

Punishment in Sweden and France

Scientific research shows that cooperation between members of a group benefits from the possibility of punishing free-riders. In addition to such 'social' punishment there is also 'antisocial' punishment whereby the interest of the group is secondary to the position of the punisher, who views the other members of the group as competitors rather than colleagues. Once again we will take a closer look at this difference by considering two detective stories and two real-life cases.

There can be no doubt that the much-loved Wallander (from Sweden) and Maigret (from France) should be seen as people who try to make a positive difference to the societies to which they belong. Both expose criminals who pose a threat to ordinary citizens. And so their work can be seen as the social punishment of people who break the social rules. This satisfies the readers' sense of justice and acts as a warning to others who consider breaking the law.

Despite all their achievements for the public cause, at times both Wallander and Maigret face opposition from the senior ranks of their own organisations. These individuals are annoyed by the popularity of their subordinates and sometimes feel the need to make the internal power relations clear. They consider their own position to be more important than the public cause. This type of behaviour can be seen as the antisocial punishment of hard-working, collaborative police officers. The immediate bosses of the two inspectors, the 'middle management,' also play an interesting role in this confrontation.

Sweden

In the story *One Step Behind*, Inspector Wallander comes up against a young chief prosecutor who becomes extremely frustrated with the experienced detective during a murder case.

'I've been expecting a debriefing for quite a while,' Thurnberg said. His voice was high-pitched and always sounded on the verge of cracking [...] 'In the future I expect to be continuously apprised of the situation without having to ask [...]'

Wallander felt no need to answer. He waited for him to continue. 'The investigation up to this point can hardly be called successful or even as thorough as one would hope,' Thurnberg said, gesturing to a long list of points he had written on a pad of paper in front of him. Wallander felt as if he was back at school being told he had failed a test.

'I'll see to it that you have my list of complaints about the handling of the case on your desk tomorrow morning,' Thurnberg said. 'I'll be expecting a written response from you.'

Wallander stared back at him quizzically. 'Do you really mean that you want us to waste time writing letters to each other while a killer who's committed five brutal murders is still running around out there?'

'What I mean is that the investigation so far has not been satisfactory.'

Wallander hit the table with his fist and got up so violently that the chair fell to the ground. [...] Wallander left the room and slammed the door behind him."

A few hours later Wallander gets a phone call from his immediate boss, Lisa Holgersson. 'I think we have a problem,' she said. 'Thurnberg spoke to me after your argument [...] He says you're not fit to be in charge of the investigation.'[9]

---

9 Mankell 2012, pp. 329–31, 333, 355–56, 445, 472.

Holgersson stays out of this power struggle. She initially refrains from taking sides and acts only as a go-between. At a press conference a few days later the two adversaries are evenly matched. 'There were many questions. Thurnberg handled most of them, with Wallander jumping in from time to time.' But when there is a brief pause, 'Wallander got up, which the others took as a signal that the conference was over. Wallander thought Thurnberg had probably intended to end it in a more formal manner.'

The confrontation is decided in Wallander's favour when he finds a promising trace of the killer. Now the boss is no longer neutral. 'This is a significant breakthrough,' she said as soon as he had sat down in a comfortable armchair across from her. 'Thurnberg is impressed.' 'Impressed by what?' 'You'll have to ask him that. But you're living up to your reputation.'

The attempt by the powerful chief prosecutor to undermine the simple inspector has failed. In this environment, where those who cooperate well can count on the support of both their colleagues and the general public, the social operator Wallander prevails over the antisocial punisher Thurnberg. Go-between Lisa is the weathervane who shows which way the balance of power is moving. At first she is neutral, but once she suspects that Wallander will get the killer, she picks his side. Despite his elevated formal position Thurnberg has no choice but to join ranks with her and Wallander.

This becomes clear at a team meeting at which the various detectives express divergent views. But in the course of the meeting Thurnberg announces that he now agrees with Wallander. It is his sole contribution to the meeting. After all, once the chief prosecutor has declared his backing for Wallander, there is not much left to discuss. The ranks have closed and the investigation team can once more take a united approach to tackling the case.

France

In the story *Maigret on the Defensive*, Inspector Maigret of France finds himself in a similar situation to his Swedish counterpart. Out of the blue he receives a written summons to report to the Chief Commissioner's office immediately. 'He wasn't forty yet, but after school he had accumulated enough degrees to be put at the head of any administration.' The Chief Commissioner starts making conversation: 'You are very well known, Monsieur Maigret, very popular.' The voice remained so gentle that it almost seemed as though the Chief Commissioner had summoned him in order to congratulate him. 'Your methods, according to the press, are fairly spectacular [...] So you can be seen for hours on end in little bars and cafés, in thousands of places where one wouldn't expect to find an officer of your rank.'

And then the senior official gets to the point: a young woman has filed a complaint against Maigret. 'Do you know Mademoiselle Nicole Prieur? [...] You haven't heard of Monsieur Jean-Baptiste Prieur, Head of Petitions at the State Council, either?' 'No.' 'He's Nicole's uncle, and she lives with him.' This time the tone was harder and the eyes had stopped smiling. 'I'm waiting for your answer.' 'Is this an interrogation?' 'That's up to you. I asked you a question.' 'May I ask on what authority?' 'As your superior officer.' Sometime later the Chief of the Police Judiciaire, Maigret's immediate superior, breaks the bad news. 'Finally, I have to tell you about the solution that has been suggested to me [...] You're to apply for sick leave, which will last until the investigation concerning you is over.'

A few days later, by which time Maigret has managed to clear his name, the conversation is resumed. 'What can I say to you?' 'Nothing, sir.' 'Are you angry with me?' 'No...' 'I called the Chief Commissioner, who called the Minister of the Interior...' 'Who, in turn, called his friend Jean-Baptiste Prieur...' 'Probably....'[10]

As in the case of Wallander, here the highest-ranked official is not out to look after the public interest but instead puts his own position first. Antisocial punishment here means putting a successful and popular inspector in his place. However, the role of the middle management in the two stories is very different. Lisa Holgersson can afford to wait and see who comes out of the power struggle on top and then choose their side. The Chief of the Police Judiciaire does not have the same luxury; the Chief Commissioner's position is so strong, he is so far above the Chief, that the latter is nothing more than his errand boy. Maigret understands this. He himself is in a weak position vis-à-vis this *normalien* with his hotlines to the minister

---

10 Simenon (1966), pp. 16, 19, 21, 146, 186.

and other high-ranking officials. In contrast to Thurnberg, the Chief Commissioner is not damaged by his failed attempt to undermine Maigret; he can permit himself to pretend that his attempt at anti-social punishment never happened. Equally, Nicole Prieur, who seeks to discredit Maigret with her statement, goes unpunished. The fact that they are both well connected means that any charge Maigret brings against them is by definition hopeless. In this situation even support from the Chief and his colleagues will not be enough to sway the balance of power in Maigret's favour.

Is this story typical of the France of the 1960s when Simenon wrote the book, or do colleagues in a hierarchy still treat each other this way? I believe that they do, as is illustrated by a detective story of a more recent date. A computer whizz-kid called Cob has joined the Paris crime squad.

> Since he had little chance of passing the cut-throat *concours administratifs* and would have to rely on promotions based on length of service, Cob seemed perfectly content to remain a junior officer [...] Every officer in the *brigade* knew about Cob's technical wizardry, especially his immediate superiors who were suspicious initially, until they realised that he was not a threat to their positions. Having once been treated like a sort of *idiot savant* by the departments to which he was assigned, he was now considered a genius.[11]

Like Maigret's Chief Commissioner, the modern police chiefs put their own position before the general interest. Until it becomes clear that Cob poses no threat to them, their tendency is towards antisocial punishment; after all, with his capabilities he could be a threat to their positions. However, the wunderkind proves to be no fighter and shows himself willing to accept a modest role. This is not in the general interest given that Cob, with his skills, could do more good for society in a higher position than in his current junior role. As is the case with Maigret, in this police force, social punishment (finding criminals) is given less importance than its antisocial equivalent (protecting the position of those in charge).

---

11 Lemaitre (2015), p. 217.

Real-Life Events

Let us return from fiction to real life and remind ourselves of the situation surrounding the Swedish private jet scandal. Various directors of several large companies used company jets for private jaunts, for example, to attend sporting events or hunting parties. They hardly deny anything when accused of having failed to put the collective corporate interest first on these occasions. Across the country there is great pressure to restore the balance. The perpetrators come under attack from the trade unions, the Swedish Shareholder Association, the public prosecutor, accountants and opinion leaders such as the archbishop and the author Henning Mankell.

Within a few weeks the principal perpetrators have lost their jobs and the companies involved have apologised to the general public. They promise that it will never happen again and the public believe them. This clears the way for the trade unions to resume relations with the new management. Social punishment has been meted out to the perpetrators so that all parties involved can now once again take part in the joint project (to promote the interests of the company and its employees) without criticism from those they represent.

In France, labour relations are more complex. President Hollande invites employers and employees to a 'social dialogue'. In 2014, most trade unions stay away after the president announces plans to simplify the employment legislation, the 3,400-page *Code du travail*. 'Let us no longer speak of social dialogue. This is a social diktat,' as one trade union representative put it. The following year the process is no smoother following the battle between board members of Air France and protesting staff. Outraged that some of its members face prosecution, the Communist-inspired trade union CGT boycotts the meeting.

Former trade union leader Nicole Notat, of the more moderate CFDT,[12] plays down the confrontation. 'The mishap at Air France creates the impression that it has become a symbol of the entire social dialogue in France,' she said in a radio broadcast. This is incorrect because 'Air France has always been a company where social dialogue was well developed.' Guy Groux, an expert on trade unions, is more nuanced. 'In France the gap between the arrogant elite and the little

---

12 Confédération française démocratique du travail.

man is huge which is why social dialogue can get fierce at times. But truly, even here things are gradually improving.'[13]

How realistic are such optimistic assessments? Are employers and employees now better at meeting each other half way than they used to be? Are employees prepared to sacrifice wages to make the company (more) profitable and, vice versa, are employers prepared to pay for things such as training courses to enable their staff to keep up in the ever more competitive labour market? Are people willing to impose social punishment, are they inclined to invest in a shared interest? Or do the two parties continue to view each other as adversaries? In that case, initiatives that benefit everyone, such as Hollande's dialogue, will be boycotted and negotiations about salaries and other working conditions will be conducted with daggers drawn, with the stronger party dictating its solutions to the weaker one.

In September 2015, the whole of France was watching the confrontation between employers and employees in the village of Hambach in Alsace, home to the Daimler group plant that manufactures the popular Smart car. The management had asked its 800 employees to extend their 35-hour working week to 39 hours while wages would only be increased by two hours. In return, their jobs would be guaranteed for the next four years. The proposal was put to the employees for consultation. In the background was the knowledge that Daimler had opened a new plant in Slovenia to which the French production activities could quite easily be transferred and where costs were substantially lower.

The leading French unions were opposed to the plan. On the day of the vote local CFDT leader Didier Getrey handed out pamphlets claiming that the management was not legally entitled to pose this question. 'This is a test of what a major national fight over the 35-hour working week could look like,' said Getrey.

The outcome of the vote – 56 per cent of staff in favour – was met with jubilation in the press: Look, modern France is after all willing to make concessions and reach compromises! But on closer inspection it became clear there was a problem: while three-quarters of the white-collar workers had backed the proposal, 61 per cent of the factory workers had voted against. The social divide that had split France for

---

13 *NRC Handelsblad*, 19 October 2015.

so long was still very much in evidence. Getrey, backed by the CGT, continued the fight. 'If they want us to work for 39 hours and pay us for 39 hours, that is fine. But otherwise it boils down to blackmail. We will not budge a single centimetre.'

In December 2015, the company's bosses decided to press ahead, sending all employees a contract amending the 35-hour working week and guaranteeing them a job for the next five years. The deadline for signing was 18 December. If 75 per cent of staff agreed to the extended working week, it would be introduced in January. If not, 'We would clearly need to study the possibility of making this car elsewhere,' said the human resources director, adding, 'We are confident that enough people will sign.'[14]

His assessment proved accurate: the following day it was announced that 90 per cent of employees had signed. Had a spark jumped between the management and the staff, making both parties willing to make concessions in the interests of the common good? I fear not. Most of the factory workers were against the wage sacrifice they were being required to make but bowed to the threat of plant closure. The stronger party, the management, imposed its solution on the weaker one, which had no option but to yield.

Why did the trade unions CGT and CFDT reject the wage adjustment? What was their priority: the collective interest – the retention of jobs – or their own position? A position which stood to benefit from a continuation of the confrontation in which, as Didier Getrey put it, the entire country could see them fighting their members' corner. It would be hard to imagine a better marketing campaign for organisations that had been facing falling membership for years. Unlike Sweden, it would seem that France is still not the kind of country where social punishment prevails over the antisocial variety.

Conclusion

It transpires that countries with relatively high levels of corruption, where the judiciary is strongly influenced by external parties, where leaders are reluctant to delegate their responsibilities and where employers and employees spend more time fighting each other than

---

14 *New York Times*, 12 December 2015.

working together, are also the countries where antisocial punishment is more prevalent than in the countries that have better scores in these areas. The two things are connected. In countries where the population has little confidence in its leaders and institutions, crafty free-riders who play the system are more likely to be admired than punished. In all such societies, a position of high status will also bring higher rewards than in societies where those who cooperate are in the majority and free-riders are dealt with severely. In these countries social punishment results in higher investments in common projects than in countries where antisocial punishment is dominant – not just in scientific games and crime novels but also in real life.

Chapter 4

NORTHERN AND SOUTHERN EUROPE

Power Distance

In the late 1960s, Dutch social psychologist Geert Hofstede conducted a study in around 50 countries among 116,000 employees of computer company IBM. He wanted to know how they felt about their labour conditions. Why did employees in some countries see certain remuneration systems, for example bonuses, as a stimulus while the same measure had the opposite effect in other countries? In 1980, Hofstede published the results of this huge study under the title *Culture's Consequences.*[1] Hofstede concluded that cultural differences, in the sense of the differences in people's mental programming, are the main reason why people behave so differently depending on the country they are from.

This mental programming begins from a very young age when children are punished and rewarded for their behaviour, primarily by their parents. They are praised for using the potty and reprimanded for hitting their little brother. Fearing the loss of their parents' love, children gradually learn these lessons and put them into practice. After the toddler stage the child develops an internal conscience and starts applying what they have learned even when their parents are not around. At this point the child has internalised the values, meaning that it effortlessly conforms to the behaviour expected of it. Breaking these internalised rules triggers unpleasant feelings such as fear and shame. Expressions of praise and encouragement make the child feel happy and loved.[2] In this way, through trial and error, the

---

1 There have been several revised publications, for example, in 2001.
2 Forman, Aksan, Kochanska (2004).

child will conform to the prevailing value system and eventually, sub-consciously, pass this on to the next generation. Different countries have different sets of rules about what is right and wrong, resulting in new generations of Britons, Germans, French and Greeks down the centuries.

Besides our deeply held universal values, such as the right to life, different basic values can be distinguished between countries. For our purposes, we are mainly interested in the basic value that Hofstede refers to as 'power distance'. The individual countries' scores for this basic value reflect the degree to which less powerful members of the group expect and accept unequal distribution of power.[3]

The scores for the various countries in Table 4.1 show that Western Europe separates on this point into the same two blocs as we have seen in the previous chapters. Northern Europe is characterised by lower scores for power distance compared to southern Europe. This

Table 4.1 Power distance

United Kingdom	35
Ireland	28
Germany	35
Austria	11
The Netherlands	38
Sweden	31
Denmark	18
Norway	31
Northern Europe	*11–38*
Italy	50
France	68
Spain	57
Portugal	63
Greece	60
Southern Europe	*50–68*

Source: Hofstede (1980,1999).

---

3 Hofstede's research has been replicated and expanded by many other experts, including E. Meyer (2014). As I consider there are no material differences between the findings, I have limited myself to Hofstede's groundbreaking work. In addition to power distance he identifies four other basic values, which I have disregarded as they are less relevant to my argument.

means that northern Europeans assume to a greater degree than their southern neighbours that all people are equal. In many cases they will be less afraid to challenge more powerful or more senior members of the group and to give their opinion. No wonder that southern Europeans often consider their northern neighbours to be naive and outspoken. Conversely, the Northerners see those living in the southern part of the continent as cunning and devious.

In this chapter we will look at how these cultural differences make people in our 13 countries act differently. First, we will revisit the examples from the recent past that we have already discussed. Could it be that the greater levels of corruption in Italy and Spain compared to Germany and the United Kingdom could be attributable to different value systems? Might this also be the reason why labour relations in France are worse than in Sweden? And explain the difference between social and antisocial punishment? Next, we will go back in time to explore whether the cultural differences identified by Hofstede date back just a few decades or have been around for much longer. Finally, we will consider how the European divide affects economic performance and mutual cooperation.

Modern-Day National Behaviour

Like other northern European countries, Germany has a relatively low score for the basic value of power distance. That means that the German population believes that all people, regardless of their social status or background, are more or less equal. No wonder there was outrage when it transpired that Federal President Christian Wulff had taken advantage of all sorts of privileges such as a low-interest mortgage, subsidised hotel stays and cut-price car rental. According to the prevailing value system, Wulff had abused his high social position. With the press feeding public opinion with new scandals over a period of several weeks, the Federal President's position was rapidly undermined and he was forced to step down. In this universe, corruption – even on a modest scale – is not left to fester for long.

The adventures of private detective Selb and former police commissioner Nägelsbach give us an insight into how a low score for power distance affects the way people feel. Working outside the official channels, the two friends set a trap to catch a criminal. The initiative failed miserably and Nägelsbach is deeply ashamed at having operated outside the rules that apply to everyone; after all, catching criminals is a job for the police and not for private citizens. It is this feeling that causes him to want to give himself up to the authorities, even though this could result in a prison sentence. His wife backs him up in this. Later in the story, private detective Selb reacts in the same way when he realises that his client is the wanted murderer and that he has failed to expose him in time. He, too, suffers deep feelings of shame and guilt and, in order to make up for his failings, considers killing the murderer himself and accepting the consequences. Both sleuths are not just looking for a criminal but for a clear conscience as well. Their lives are based on the notion that all people are equal and that those who break the rules should be punished. This applies not just to the killer but to them, too. Ultimately both decide, albeit with a heavy heart, not to take action but their struggle with self-reproach is so intense that we can understand why people like this have little patience with corrupt government officials and others who do not stick to the rules that apply to everyone in their country.

In an earlier chapter we compared corruption in Germany to the situation in Spain, a country where people in positions of power, be they real-life football club presidents such as Núñez and Pérez or fictional ones such as Basté, are always out to maintain or strengthen their position. The table shows that Spain has a relatively high score for power distance; this implies that the average Spaniard accepts that social differences between people exist and is inclined to behave in accordance with the wishes of those in power.

In the real-life as well as the fictional situations cited, the club directors are so sure of their position that with no twinges of conscience whatsoever they commit tax fraud, sell a training ground to the province at a vastly inflated price and bring a small club into financial difficulties so they can snap up their ground cheaply. Furthermore, scientific research shows that many mayors and other local bigwigs like to reward those who support them by getting them a job in local government.

Not everyone is willing to accept this state of affairs. When detective Pepe Carvalho finds out about the plans of club president and former mayor of Barcelona Basté, he wants to charge him. But the way things are in Spain, Pepe's chances are slim. The great power distance means that others who are aware of the situation are afraid that Basté and his friends will find a way of punishing them if they testify against them or cross them in some other way. As a result, certain private individuals in positions of power have more influence on people's behaviour than public authorities like the police or the judiciary. After all, when push comes to shove, police officers and judges will also bow to the wishes of the elite.

Elsewhere we compared labour relations in France to those in Sweden. Could it be that the behaviour displayed by employers and employees in these countries can also be explained by the different scores for power distance?

In France the management teams of Air France and the Smart plant in Alsace meet to discuss cost cuts. In a society characterised by large power differences, they feel secure in their position. Based on this feeling, they propose wage cuts along with the threat of job losses. Especially staff in lower-paid positions and the unions that represent them view this behaviour by the ruling elite as threatening and humiliating, triggering strong feelings of anger and fear. At Charles de Gaulle airport these spiral into a physical assault on the management, and in Alsace the wage offer is only accepted once the threat of mass redundancies is looming very large. The confrontations do nothing to improve the traditionally tense labour relations, which is why President Hollande has so little success with his social dialogue.

In Sweden, employers and employees clash when it becomes known that directors of several large companies have abused their position by using corporate jets for private outings. The general public (represented by parties such as the unions), the investigating judge and the church – everyone is up in arms. The behaviour of the various directors flies in the face of the deep-rooted notion that all people are equal. The confrontation is short but intense. The directors involved are sacked, the companies make public apologies and appoint new directors. The unions and other organisations can now be confident in resuming their cooperation with the new boards. In hindsight, the scandal caused no more than a temporary ripple in the labour relations and before long the conflict-avoidance model regained its familiar dominance.

At the level of the individual we saw how Inspector Maigret gets a much harder time from his superior than his Swedish counterpart

Wallander. In both cases those in power are irked by the success of their subordinates and want to teach them a lesson. Both sleuths manage to get out of this awkward situation by tracking down the criminals. In France, where hierarchical distances are great as reflected by the high score for power distance, the chief commissioner has the luxury of pretending that nothing has happened; his attack has failed, but he will suffer no permanent damage or loss of reputation as a result.

In Sweden, the position of those in high places is less comfortable. While the chief prosecutor stops short of giving Wallander a formal apology he does suffer the humiliation of having to rejoin the investigative team which, led by his adversary, continues along the same track. Low power distance means that the other members of the team take little notice of the rivals' formal positions; the position within the team and the informal power relations are what really matter here.

The role of middle management in these confrontations is also interesting. People in this position within a hierarchy will seek to side with the strongest party. In France the Chief Commissioner's position is so untouchable that Maigret's immediate superior, the Chief of the Police Judiciaire, has no option but to choose his side. Maigret understands this completely and accepts his apologies. By contrast, Wallander's chief Lisa Holgersson can permit herself to withhold her support from the higher-ranking chief prosecutor without the latter being able to punish her for this. While formally he is ranked higher than her, informally, in terms of basic values, everyone is equal. When it subsequently becomes clear that the chief prosecutor is set to lose the argument, she chooses to back the lower-ranked Wallander and the chief prosecutor bites the dust.

We could review the other examples – delegating in the workplace, the functioning of the judiciary, styles of cooperation and punishment in the various northern and southern European countries – in a similar way, but that would result in a tedious summary. In general, we can conclude that relationships in southern Europe are characterised by greater power differences than in the north of the continent. In the south, the higher scores for this basic value cause strong feelings of anxiety and impotent rage on the part of the weaker party in all kinds of situations, making cooperation with those in higher places more problematic. More corruption, more antisocial punishment and less freedom for subordinates are the result. Has this difference between northern and southern Europe come about in recent decades or are we dealing with a genuine culture gap that dates back to the distant past? In other words: is the difference temporary or structural?

Two Cultural Regions

The Romans

The first laws of the Roman Empire were announced around 450 BC by means of 12 stone plaques, known as tables, displayed in the city. The articles, which were not easy to interpret, all related to what was or was not permitted along with the relevant sanction (see Table 4.2). The only exception was table VIII.4, which stated: 'If a patron shall have devised any deceit against his client, let him be accursed.'[4]

This article is proof that even at this very early stage in Roman history there were at least two separate groups of citizens. The 'patrons' were the leaders of the most influential families. Also known as *patres familias*, they were locked in a permanent mutual power struggle. To succeed they needed the support of less distinguished persons. These were their 'clients' who, in return, could count on assistance from their patrons.

Such relationships based on mutual dependency continued to exist in subsequent centuries after Rome became a republic and grew into a great empire. Now the *patres* needed support in order to be elected to various public offices. In 64 BC, Marcus Tullius Cicero, the great orator and writer, stood for election as consul. His brother Quintus wrote Marcus a letter, giving him advice on how to behave

Table 4.2 Power distance Latin/Germanic

LATIN	50–68
GERMANIC	11–38

Source: Hofstede (1980, 1999).

---

4 The original Twelve Tables have not survived. Copies of various sections of text have been discovered at several sites, enabling the reconstruction of the full text (Crawford, 1996). The quotes appearing in this text are sourced from the translation by J. S. Arkenberg (Internet Ancient History Sourcebook).

if his campaign was to be successful. 'Your attendants can also be divided into three groups: (1) those who come to your home for the morning salutation, (2) those who escort you from your home, and (3) those who follow you through the city.'[5] The morning salute, in Latin *salutatio*, was a ritual whereby clients gathered at the home of their patron to bid him good morning, thus publicly displaying their esteem for the latter's superior position. After the *salutatio* the patron would make for the Forum. Quintus advised as follows:

> Come down to the Forum at the same time every day; for a large crowd of escorts every day brings you great renown and great respect [...] those whose age and occupation will allow it should attend you constantly, but those who cannot personally attend you should assign their relatives to this duty. I strongly urge, and I think it important, that you always appear with a group of attendants.[6]

The more time and effort Cicero's clients put into his election campaign, the more Cicero owed them in return. This debt would have to be repaid eventually, for example, by bestowing certain government positions after his election. Romans of all ranks and stations understood and accepted that patrons repaid their debt to their clients in this way.

Clients, in turn, had to consider carefully who to lend their support to. Obviously they stood to receive better rewards from a successful patron than from a candidate who was defeated. This is why the size of a patron's following was so important and why it must be on public display: it enabled both other patrons and potential clients to gauge a person's public esteem, in Latin *existimatio*.

A few decades later, Julius Caesar's adoptive son Octavian succeeded in placing the entire Roman Empire under his sole rule. The patronage system continued to operate under Emperor Augustus, as Octavian called himself, and his successors. The poet Martial described the relationship between patron and client in the first century AD. 'Yesterday, *Caecilianus*, when I came to bid you

---

5 Shelton (1998), p. 218.
6 Ibid., pp. 218–19.

"Good Morning", I accidentally greeted you by name and forgot to call you *"My Lord"*. *How much did this liberty cost me? You knocked a hundred quadrantes off my allowance.*[7] It is clear that a client had to act cautiously if he was to avoid offending his patron and pay tribute to him in the required manner. Given that the client was financially dependent on his patron it was easy for the latter to punish him, with the amount withheld exactly commensurate with the extent of the patron's displeasure.

There were many different ways of humiliating clients. 'While you are drinking pints of deep purple wine, Cotta, and guzzling rich dark Opimian, you set before me Sabine wine which has just been made. And then you ask me, "Do you want a gold wine goblet?" Who wants a gold goblet for lead wines?'[8] You do not need to be a connoisseur of Roman wines to understand that the wine being served to the client is of considerably poorer quality than what his patron is drinking. The latter plays with the situation by offering his client a nice glass; this costs him nothing. The result is contempt for one party and impotent rage for the other.

The pater familias was not only superior to his clients; his children's position was even weaker. A contemporary of Martial, the philosopher and pedagogue Seneca, emphasised the importance of obedience, in Latin *pietas*.

How great an achievement it is [...] to be able to say: 'I obeyed my parents; I deferred to their authority, whether it was fair or unfair or even harsh; I showed myself compliant and submissive.'[9]

Even after the children had grown up the power of the father, in Latin *patria potestas*, remained virtually unlimited. For example the father had the right to ban those who did not conform to his will from his home, in Latin *abdicatio*. While this was not a formal legal right, the custom was a means by which the pater familias could exert pressure. Sons and daughters needed their father's permission

---

7 Martial 6.88 quoted in Shelton (1998), p. 14.
8 Shelton, J.-A. (1998), p. 317.
9 Shelton (1998), p. 31.

to marry. The threat of paternal intervention was always present. Marriage provided no escape; the pater familias was permitted to beat members of his family and lock them up.

Although it is not possible for us to interview the Romans who lived in the centuries around the beginning of our era as Hofstede was able to do with the IBM employees, these examples strongly suggest that Roman society was characterised by relatively high scores for the basic value of power distance. For the sake of comparison, let us consider the Germanic value system in place at this time.

The Ancient Germans

The earliest-known Germanic tribes lived in the Baltic region in the second millennium BC and made their livelihoods by a combination of primitive crop cultivation and livestock farming. They would burn sections of forest and use the fertile ash to grow various crops. When the soil became depleted they would move on and burn down another piece of forest. The livestock, mainly cattle, pigs and goats, were left to forage for food.

After around 1,000 BC this semi-nomadic existence started to change.[10] Excavations show Germanic peoples increasingly settling in permanent villages consisting of 5–10 farmsteads. The villages were surrounded by small fields that were cultivated for extended periods. The soil was kept fertile by using the manure produced by the livestock. Crops included grains such as oats, rye and wheat as well as beans and peas, with the diet being supplemented with the produce of the hunt and wild fruits.

Most years all of the produce was needed to sustain the community. There was no such thing as economic specialisation; all villagers were farmers. Favourable weather conditions and a good harvest allowed modest reserves to be built, which could then be traded with itinerant merchants for iron weapons and tools. A poor harvest meant people went hungry and if this situation became chronic, part of the population would have no option but to move away in search of new arable land.

---

10 Hedeager (1992), p. 217.

The 'lord' of such a village was called a *frô*. He was responsible for his wife, children, slaves and other dependents. *Frô* can also mean 'chieftain'.[11] The Roman writer Tacitus, whose *Germania* was published in 98 AD, often uses the plural of the term, in Latin *principes,* in order to denote that Germanic chieftains frequently teamed up to take a leading role in the public assembly, were collectively responsible for passing justice and shared tributes.

Not all tribes had this style of political organisation; some had a tribal king. Which is why Tacitus writes of 'the king or the chieftain' and 'the king or the leader.'[12] What is striking is that all these leaders were elected by the free male members of the tribe at the public assembly. The fact that they were elected implies that they did not wield absolute power, whatever their title. After all, they could always be ousted. Tacitus gives a detailed description of the decision-making process at a public assembly.[13]

On affairs of smaller moment, the chiefs consult; on those of greater importance, the whole community [...] An inconvenience produced by their liberty is, that they do not all assemble at a stated time, as if it were in obedience to a command; but two or three days are lost in the delays of convening. When they all think fit, they sit down armed. Silence is proclaimed by the priests [...] Then the king, or chief, and such others as are conspicuous for age, birth, military renown, or eloquence, are heard; and gain attention rather from their ability to persuade, than their authority to command. If a proposal displease, the assembly reject by an inarticulate murmur; if it prove agreeable, they clash their javelins; for the most honourable expression of assent among them is the sound of arms.[14]

---

11 Green (1998), pp. 106, 115.
12 Tacitus (2009), pp. 67–68.
13 In many Germanic languages the word for a public assembly is 'Thing'. This root word is still recognisable in 'Folketing', the name for the Danish parliament, as well as in the Norwegian 'Stortinget' and the Icelandic 'Althing'.
14 Tacitus (2009), pp. 67–68.

This quote shows that by Roman standards those attending the assembly had little respect for their leaders. They showed up when they felt like it and gave their opinion with no regard for rank or station. Tacitus continues in amazement: 'These people, naturally void of artifice or disguise, disclose the most secret emotions of their hearts in the freedom of festivity. The minds of all being thus displayed without reserve.'[15] Stating frankly and candidly what was really on their mind was the very last thing a Roman citizen would consider doing in company, instead thinking very carefully about what was safe to say to whom to avoid offending someone more powerful.

Who took part in the public assembly? All men permitted to bear arms, the freemen, were obliged to attend and had the right to speak. The word for freedom (Old High German: *frítuam*, Old English: *frēodōm*) originally designated the legal privilege of self-judgement enjoyed by a freeman, hence the status of a freeman.[16] There was no reason why they had to adhere to rules and laws; if they did so it was of their own free will. Tacitus describes an extreme example.

> What is extraordinary, they play at dice, when sober, as a serious business: and that with such a desperate venture of gain or loss, that, when everything else is gone, they set their liberties and persons on the last throw. The loser goes into voluntary servitude: and, though the youngest and strongest, patiently suffers himself to be bound and sold. Such is their obstinacy in a bad practice – they themselves call it honor.[17]

Despite the fact that there were no official authorities to enforce this, the loser would still enter slavery. Having willingly submitted to the rules of the game, he considered he had no other option. After all, all freemen were equal; why should an exception be made for him? Would that not be unfair towards those who did respect the agreements? He would not want that on his conscience and would prefer to accept his punishment voluntarily. The tribe was more

---

15 Tacitus (2009), p. 75.
16 Green (1998), pp. 41–42.
17 Tacitus (2009), p. 75.

important than personal interest. By Roman standards the Germanic peoples did not only have little respect for authority but in fact a complete lack of understanding of unequal power relations between fellow members of the tribe. 'The Germani in particular lacked any sense of obedience, military or otherwise, including even a word for this concept so foreign to them.'[18] People cooperated – in the family, clan, raiding party and tribe, based on mutual loyalty. This cooperation was voluntary; nobody was so fearful of more powerful people that they could be forced. This behaviour would suggest lower scores for power distance than those applicable to the Roman Empire.

Did this difference between the Germanic and Latin value systems diminish in subsequent centuries or does it persist to this day?

Early Middle Ages (400–1000 AD)

Following the fall of the Roman Empire in the fifth century AD, the Latin value system continued in the monastic system which experienced rapid growth in this period. In 529, Benedict of Nursia founded the monastery of Monte Cassino. The Rule he introduced for the monastery was to gain much following in subsequent centuries. The form was new but the content sounds familiar.[19]

> Chapter 5: The first degree of humility is obedience without delay [...] on account of the holy servitude they have professed, whether through fear of hell or on account of the glory of life eternal. As soon as any order has been given by a superior, as being the same as if the order were divinely given, they can brook no delay in carrying it out.
>
> Chapter 71: And if any brother is corrected, it matters not in what way, by the abbot or by any other of those senior to him, or if he shall at all perceive that any senior's mind is angered or moved against him, however slightly, at once without delay having prostrated on the ground let him lie at his feet, thus making satisfaction until that feeling be healed by giving of

---

18 Green (1998), p. 69.
19 All quotes here sourced from //www.solesmes.com/sites/default/files/upload/pdf/rule_of_st_benedict.pdf.

benediction. But if anyone should disdain to do so, either let him be subjected to corporal punishment, or else if he be contumacious let him be expelled from the monastery.

Thus the Latin value system exacting obedience was cast in a new, Christian form. The authority of the abbot, who replaced the pater familias, was further boosted by the realisation that he was a vessel of God's will. Consequently, the resulting behaviour is quintessentially Roman. The believer must not only obey but also do so in a way that pleases the authority in question; the form is just as important as the content. Mutual solidarity among the members of the group, so important in Germanic relations, is not allowed.

Chapter 69: Precautions must be taken lest on any occasion one monk in the monastery presume to constitute himself the patron of another, or as it were to take him under his care, even although they be related by the tie of near kinship. Let no monk presume to do such a thing in any way whatever, because therefrom can arise very grave occasion of scandal. But if anyone shall have transgressed in this respect, let him be somewhat sharply punished. (Benedict, Chapter 69)

Seeking protection in the group was forbidden in monasteries that followed the Rule of Benedict. Clearly, this ban bolstered the position of those in power.

In the fifth century AD the Roman Empire suffered Germanic invasions not only on the continent but also in what is now Great Britain. The south and east of the British Isles were invaded by Angles, Saxons and Jutes from what is now northern Germany and Jutland. They established hundreds of small kingdoms and forced the natives out to the west. Nowhere in the former Roman Empire suffered such severe social decline as here. By around 410 AD, money transactions had disappeared completely and with stone construction unknown to the invaders, cities and villas around the country soon fell into disrepair and were replaced by wooden structures.

The most important surviving work from this period is the *Ecclesiastical History of the English People* written by the Venerable Bede. This chronicler was born around 673 AD in Northumbria and spent his entire life in the northeast of England. His work, which appeared in 731 AD, starts with the earliest known inhabitants of the island and continues up until Bede's own time. Unsurprisingly Christianisation features prominently in this work. In 627 AD, Edwin, the king of Northumbria, was considering converting to Christianity.

> When the king had heard his words, he answered that he was both willing and bound to receive the faith [...] He said, however, that he would confer about this with his loyal chief men and his counsellors so that, if they agreed with him, they might all be consecrated together in the waters of life [...] Coifi, the chief the priests, answered at once:[...] So it follows that if, on examination these new doctrines which have now been explained to us, are found to be better and more effectual, let us accept them at once without any delay.[20]

The need to consult with others, openly voice their opinion and take a joint decision is wholly consistent with the Germanic tradition. The church steadily expanded its position in Britain. In 669 AD, the pope appointed Theodore of Tarsus, who was a monk in Rome, Archbishop of Canterbury. Four years later Theodore summoned a council of bishops together with many teachers of the church. Bede described the gathering. 'When they were assembled he began, as befitted an archbishop, by charging them to observe diligently all those things which were conducive to the unity and peace of the church. The text of the decisions of the synod is as follows:

> Chapter 4: That monks shall not wander from place to place, that is to say, from monastery to monastery, unless they have letters dimissory from their own abbot; but they are to remain under that obedience which they promised at the time of their profession.
> Chapter 5: That no clergy shall leave their own bishop to wander about at will; nor shall one be received anywhere without letters commendatory from their own bishop. If he has

---

20 Bede (1969), Book II.13.

once been received and is unwilling to return when summoned, both the receiver and received shall suffer excommunication.[21]

What we have here is a frontal collision between the Latin and Germanic value systems. In the Anglican church individuals were permitted to decide for themselves where they wished to stay, with the leaders, bishops and abbots respecting this behaviour on the part of their subordinates. In the Latin tradition this was unthinkable. The freedom of movement of all members of the organisation was set in stone and any deviation had to be sanctioned by the hierarchy. In this case this applies to both the itinerant monk and the abbot who was prepared to look the other way; both took an oath of obedience which the new archbishop is now holding them to.

Inevitably, sooner or later someone falls foul. 'Not long afterwards, Archbishop Theodore, displeased by some act of disobedience of Winfrith, bishop of the Mercians, deposed him from the bishopric which he had only held a few years [...] Winfrith after his deposition retired to his own monastery of Barrow and there lived a very holy life until his death.'[22] Clearly, Theodore wanted to set an example. While Bede does not risk criticising him, he backs Winfrith by stating that he went on to lead a good life. In this way clerics with a Germanic background were forced to conform to an organisation based on the Latin value system.

Away from the church, normal life continued. In one of the many battles of these uncertain times a young thane named Imma was wounded and taken prisoner. Bede describes how he pretends he is a poor peasant who was forced to help provision the fighters. Nevertheless, his noble conqueror takes Imma prisoner.

When he had been a prisoner with the *gesith* for some time, those who watched him closely realized by his appearance, his bearing and his speech that he was not of common stock as he had said, but of noble family. Then the *gesith* called him aside and asked him very earnestly to declare his origin, promising that no harm should come to him, provided that he told him

---

21 Bede (1969), Book IV.5.
22 Bede (1969), Book IV.6.

plainly who he was. The prisoner did so, revealing that he had been one of the king's thegns. The *gesith* answered: 'I realized by every one of your answers that you were not a peasant, and now you ought to die because all my brothers and kinsmen were killed in the battle: but I will not kill you for I do not intend to break my promise.'

As soon as Imma had recovered the *gesith* sold him to a Frisian in London, but he could neither be bound on his way there nor by the Frisian […] as his master realized that he could not be bound, he gave him leave to ransom himself if he could. […] So having sworn that he would either return or send his master the money for the ransom, he went to King Hlothhere of Kent […] he asked for and received the money from him for his ransom and sent it to his master as he had promised.'[23] Once again, the Germanic honesty is striking in these stories. The thane who captures Imma could kill him but refrains from doing so because of the promise he has made. Later, Imma promises the trader to return or send the ransom money. He does the latter, even though the trader has no means of forcing him to. This does not surprise Bede; it would appear that strict adherence to agreements – which Romans would probably consider naive – was customary in this part of the world. This difference is a consequence of the different scores for power distance. In the Latin world, where the scores are high, obedience is enforced by a stronger party. In Germanic countries such behaviour is counter-productive; the stronger parties have to persuade the weaker ones to choose their side voluntarily. Such a strategy is based on the notion that all members of the group are equal. (Bede, Book IV, p. 22)

Middle Ages (1000–1500 AD)

Having determined that the Latin and Germanic value systems survived the tumultuous period following the collapse of the Roman Empire, we are now ready to move on to the Middle Ages. Were both

---

23 Bede (1969), Book IV.22.

value systems still demonstrably present in northern and southern Europe during this period? I believe that they were and wish to demonstrate this by comparing two versions of the same story, taken down in the fourteenth century by the Englishman Geoffrey Chaucer and the Italian Giovanni Boccaccio.

Equality between man and wife is a major theme in Chaucer's *The Canterbury Tales*. One of his stories tells of the young knight Arveragus who conducts a lengthy courtship of the beautiful Lady Dorigen. Eventually with success.

> But in the end she saw his worthiness …
> that privately she fell into accord
> and took him for her husband and her lord
> The lordship husbands have upon their wives.
> And to enhance the bliss of both their lives
> He freely gave his promise as a knight
> That he would never darken her delight
> By exercising his authority
> against her will…[24]

Like his Germanic ancestors, Chaucer assumes that oppression does not make for good mutual relations. Arveragus keeps his promise and so the spouses are happy together. But after about a year the knight has to leave 'to go and seek high deeds of arms and reputation in honour,' leaving Lady Dorigan behind. She then meets a squire called Aurelius, who falls in love with her. So as not to disappoint him, she sets him an impossible task which he must perform in order to win her love. However, with the aid of a magician he manages to fulfil the task. Dorigen owns up to her husband about what has happened. The knight responds as follows:

> All may be well, but you must keep your word.
> For, as may God be merciful to me,
> I rather would be stabbed than live to see
>   You fail in truth. The very love I bear you

---

24 Chaucer (1951), p. 427.

> Bids you keep truth, in that it cannot spare you.
> Truth is the highest thing in a man's keeping.[25]

So Arveragus decides that his wife may not break her promise; staying true to a promise is a matter of honour to him. This behaviour is reminiscent of various other examples from other periods in which people consider a clear conscience to be more important than their own interest. That conscience is partly shaped by the Germanic value system, in which rules that apply to everyone are considered more important than personal relationships. In this case Arveragus considers the promise his wife has made of greater importance than their relationship.

In his version of the story in the *Decameron* the Italian Boccaccio also considers this motivation. However, he has the husband Arveragus add another important argument.

> Albeit I'm also moved by my fear of the magician, for Messer Ansaldo might ask him to harm us if you played him for a fool. I therefore want you to go to him, and using any means at your disposal, I want you to do what you can to preserve your chastity and get him to release you from your promise. However, if that's not possible, then just this once you may yield your body, but not your heart, to him.[26]

In this version the husband's decision is determined by his fear of a powerful adversary. His behaviour is rooted in the Latin value system where power differences are highly significant. Confrontations trigger feelings of fear in the weaker party, who is therefore inclined to give in. Self-interest is more important than keeping a promise. This is also apparent from his instruction to his wife that she should try to talk her way out of her obligation. After all, if Ansaldo allows this, he will be unlikely to turn to the magician to exact revenge from the couple. This behaviour is based on a rational assessment of the power differences between the two parties.

---

25 Ibid., p. 447.
26 Boccaccio (2015), p. 659.

The Modern Era (1500–1900 AD)

In the subsequent centuries, obedience based on major power differences between individuals continued to play a crucial role in Latin countries. The transference of these values after the Middle Ages is easy to trace in France, where successive royal houses succeeded in establishing absolute rule. This power monopoly reached its height under Louis XIV who, on assuming sole power at the age of 24 in 1661, left his ministers in no doubt as to what he expected of them.

> It is now time that I govern them myself. You will assist me with your counsels when I ask for them. I request and order you to seal no orders except by my command [...] I order you not to sign anything, not even a passport [...] without my command.[27]

Both courtiers and official were expected just to obey orders, keeping their opinion to themselves unless the king asked for it. For Louis the purpose of his reign was not the well-being of his subjects but his own position. He describes this aim in his *Mémoires*. 'The love of glory (*la gloire*) assuredly takes precedence over all other passions in my soul [...] the hot blood of my youth and the violent desire I had to heighten my reputation instilled in me a strong passion for action; but at the same time I realized that the love of glory requires the same delicacy, if I may say so, the same sort of timidity as the most tender of passions.'[28]

Jacques-Bénigne Bossuet, court preacher and tutor to the crown prince, converted these personal notes into more general terms.

> Rulers then act as the ministers of God and as his lieutenants on earth. It is through them that God exercises his empire [...] Kings should be guarded as holy things, and whosoever neglects to protect them is worthy of death [...] Look at the prince in his cabinet. Thence go out the orders which cause the magistrates and the captains, the citizens and the soldiers, the provinces and the armies on land and on sea, to work in concert. He is the image of God, who, seated on his throne high in the heavens,

---

27 Erlanger (2003), p. 133.
28 Elias (1997), p. 194.

makes all nature move. [...] But kings, although their power comes from on high, as has been said, should not regard themselves as masters of that power to use it at their pleasure; [...] they must employ it with fear and self-restraint, as a thing coming from God and of which God will demand an account.[29]

The obligation to obey the ruler, deeply rooted in the conscience of his subjects, reminds us of the position of the strict pater familias during the Roman Empire. The author Jean de la Bruyère, a contemporary of Louis XIV, makes this comparison when he remarks 'that king rules well who makes a court and even a whole realm like a single family united under the same head.'[30]

This philosophy of life was also found outside noble circles, as can be seen from the work of Jean-Jacques Rousseau which has continued to influence the French style of education right up to the present day.[31] His book *Emile or On Education* (1762) was particularly influential. In it, Rousseau describes how he as a tutor educates a child. Emile is taught to accept authority from birth. The lessons continue as follows when he has reached the toddler stage.

If there is something he should not do, do not forbid him, but prevent him without explanation or reasoning; what you give him, give it at his first word without prayers or entreaties, above all without conditions. Give willingly, refuse unwillingly, but let your refusal be irrevocable; let no entreaties move you; let your "No", once uttered, be a wall of brass, against which the child may exhaust his strength some five or six times, but in the end he will try no more to overthrow it. Thus you will make him patient, equable, calm, and resigned, even when he does not get all he wants [...] there is no middle course; you must either make no demands on him at all, or else you must fashion him to perfect obedience. The worst education of all is to leave him hesitating between his own will and yours, constantly disputing

---

29 Bossuet (1709), history. hanover.edu.
30 Elias (1997), p. 64.
31 In 2012, American journalist Pamela Druckerman, whose children were born and are being raised in Paris, wrote: 'The modern French idea of how to parent starts with Rousseau.' (p. 101)

whether you or he is master; I would rather a hundred times that he were master.[32]

The latter remark should be taken with a pinch of salt. Further on in in his treatise Rousseau qualifies his opinion.

> Take the opposite course with your pupil; let him always think he is master while you are really master. There is no subjection so complete as that which preserves the forms of freedom; it is thus that the will itself is taken captive. Is not this poor child, without knowledge, strength, or wisdom, entirely at your mercy? Are you not master of his whole environment so far as it affects him? Cannot you make of him what you please? His work and play, his pleasure and pain, are they not, unknown to him, under your control? No doubt he ought only to do what he wants, but he ought to want to do nothing but what you want him to do.[33]

Without realising it, the child is being taught unconditional obedience. His freedom is strictly limited to the space allowed him by his educator. Subtly Rousseau teaches his pupil inner acceptance of power differences. Given this philosophy it comes as no surprise that he has no time for the British educational methods being propagated by John Locke.

> 'Reason with children' was Locke's great maxim; it is in the height of fashion at present [...] If children understood reason they would not need education; but by talking to them from their earliest age in a language they do not understand you accustom them to be satisfied with words, to question all that is said to them, to think themselves as wise as their teachers; you train them to be argumentative and rebellious; and whatever you think you gain from motives of reason, you really gain from greediness, fear, or vanity with which you are obliged to reinforce your reasoning.[34]

---

32 Rousseau (2006), p. 116.
33 Ibid., pp. 143–44.
34 Ibid., p. 114.

The lack of understanding was mutual, as is apparent from the work of Rousseau's British contemporary Laurence Sterne, whose hero Tristram Shandy travels around France. At one stage Tristram is stopped.

> It was a commissary, sent to me from the post office, with a rescript in his hand for the payment of some six livres odd sous. Upon what account? said I. – 'Tis upon the part of the king, replied the commissary, heaving up both his shoulders. – But it is an indubitable verity, continued I, […] that I owe the king of France nothing but my goodwill. – *Pardonnez moi*, replied the commissary, you are indebted to him six livres four sous for the next post from hence to St Fons, in your route to Avignon. – But I don't go by land; said I. – You may if you please; replied the commissary – I travel by water – I am going down the Rhône this very afternoon […] and I have actually paid nine livres for my passage. – *'C'est tout égal'* – 'tis all one; said he. – *Bon Dieu!* What, pay for the way I go! And for the way I do not go! […] Oh England! England! Thou land of liberty, and climate of good sense, thou tenderest of mothers.[35]

No wonder that trade in France was slow to develop with toll being levied in this way. Tristram Shandy does not understand that to the French, economic disadvantages do not weigh up to the political importance of every traveller realising that the king reigns supreme in all of France.

The differences in power distance between Britain and France also play a role in another book by Laurence Sterne, *A Sentimental Journey through France and Italy*. The main character Yorick quickly realises how he must conduct himself in Paris in order to avoid losing his place at dinner parties to a more entertaining guest. Of Yorick's encounter with a womanising marquis he writes the following:

> He could like to take a trip to England, and asked much of the English ladies. – Stay where you are, I beseech you, Mons. Le Marquis, said I – Les Messrs. Anglois can scarce get a kind

---

35 Sterne (2004), pp. 621, 624.

look from them as it is. – The Marquis invited me to supper. Mons. P*** the 'farmer general' was just as inquisitive about our taxes. – They were very considerable, he heard. – If we knew but how to collect them, said I, making him a low bow […] For three weeks together I was of every man's opinion. – *Pardi! ce Mons. Yorick a autant d'esprit que nous autres. – Il raisonne bien*, said another. – *C'est un bon enfant*, said a third. – And at this price I could have eaten and drank and been merry all the days of my life at Paris; but 'twas a dishonest *reckoning* – I grew ashamed of it – it was the gain of a slave – every sentiment of honour revolted against it – the higher I got, the more I was forced upon my *beggarly system* – the better the *Coterie* – the more children of Art – I languish'd for those of Nature: and one night, after a most vile prostitution of myself to half a dozen different people, I grew sick – went to bed – order'd La Fleur to get me horses in the morning to set out for Italy.[36]

Yorick's social skills are good enough to gain him acceptance in the salons of Paris. However, his Germanic background means that he struggles with acting the sycophantic courtier on a daily basis. This inner conflict produces feelings of guilt which persist until he removes himself from this setting. This allows him to escape the environment of the salons where he must constantly gauge the position of everyone he meets and to return to living in accordance with 'nature' where everyone is equal.

It is not hard to trace evidence of the differences in Latin and Germanic basic values through to the nineteenth century. I will limit myself to the author Madame De Staël, banished from Paris by Napoleon in 1802 because of her support of the Ancien Régime. She spent the next few years travelling extensively around the German Empire. She reported her findings in 1813 under the title *Germany*, in which she compared the two countries on many points from a French perspective. She was especially interested in the national character.

The Germans are, generally speaking, both sincere and faithful; they seldom forfeit their word, and deceit is foreign to them. If

---

36 Sterne (2004), pp. 173, 177.

this fault should ever introduce itself into Germany, it could only be through the ambition of imitating foreigners, of evincing an equal dexterity [...] It is, I believe, easy to shew that, without morality, all is danger and darkness. Nevertheless there has often been observed among the Latin nations a singularly dextrous policy in the art of emancipating themselves from every duty; but it may be said, to the glory of the German nation, that she is almost incapable of that practiced suppleness which makes all truths bend to all interests, and sacrifices every engagement to every calculation.'[37]

This German faithfulness and sincerity stems from the Germanic tradition in which power differences are less pronounced than in southern Europe. In order to limit the consequences of a steep hierarchy, the Latin tradition developed a suppleness and agility of mind that the Germans were unable to match. Madame de Staël found the relatively low score for the basic value of power distance even at the grandest court of the German Empire.

These grandees of Vienna, the most illustrious and the most wealthy in Europe, abuse none of the advantages they possess; they allow the humblest hackney coaches to stop their brilliant equipages. The Emperor and his brothers even quietly keep their place in the string, and choose to be considered, in their amusements, as private individuals; they make use of their privileges only when they fulfil their duties.[38]

In the public space everyone is expected to behave according to the rules that apply to everyone, with the social position of the road users being irrelevant. This passage suggests that the emperor and the nobility willingly submit to this kind of limitation. Madame de Staël describes the Latin peoples, including their cultural roots dating back two millennia, as follows. 'The people of those regions [...] like their founders, the Romans, they alone know how to practice the arts of dominion.' Whereas she makes the following observation with regard

---

37 Staël (1813), p. 47.
38 Ibid., p. 67.

to the peoples of Germanic origin. 'They were all distinguished, from the earliest times, by their independence and loyalty; they have ever been good and faithful.'[39]

The Twentieth Century

Our search for our Germanic and Latin roots has brought us to the first half of the Twentieth century. It is 1924 and the president of the German Reichsbank Hjalmar Schacht is on a visit to Paris to discuss the German reparations in the aftermath of the Great War. After a meeting with the chairman of the reparations commission Louis Barthou, Schacht is summoned to call on the president of the Republic Monsieur Millerand. Not to be outdone, Prime Minister Poincaré instructs Barthou to tell Schacht he must also pay a visit to this important politician.

> 'But Herr Schacht, you can understand that since you have called on Monsieur Millerand, Monsieur Poincaré attached considerable importance to a visit from you. Monsieur Poincaré is head of the government and therefore cannot simply over-look the fact that, while you have called on the President of the Republic, you ignore the head of the government.' 'I haven't the slightest intention of ignoring Monsieur Poincaré [...] But I am here once and for all as a businessman [...] and I have nothing to do with politics.' 'But you don't understand, Herr Schacht! Monsieur Poincaré insists on seeing you.' 'Then let him send for me.' 'He can't possibly do that.'[40]

French political relations in the Fourth Republic were such that the president and the prime minister were locked in a continuous power struggle. So as not to lose face as a result of being ignored by an important foreign visitor, Poincaré felt obliged to meet Schacht. To make the relationship between them absolutely clear he also wanted Schacht to approach him to request an audience rather than issuing an invitation. However, Schacht had no time for such ramifications

---

39 Ibid., pp. 37–38.
40 Schacht (1955), p. 261.

of the greater power distance in France and at first simply refused. But once he had given in, the confrontation continued. 'I waited five minutes; I waited ten minutes. I began to grow impatient and waited another five minutes [...] Then my patience gave out. I saw no reason to put up with discourtesy, even from the French Prime Minister.'[41]

According to a value system in which all people are considered equal regardless of their position, the treatment Schacht was made to endure was humiliating and incomprehensible to him. But for his host, who was acting in accordance with the Latin value system, being kept waiting was an important part of the meeting as it makes everyone aware of where they all stand in the pecking order.

Conclusion

The different approaches to power differences in northern and southern Europe go back a long way. The clash which started with the Roman Empire and the Germanic tribes around 2,000 years ago still carries on today. The border between the two cultural regions still largely follows the old border, the *limes*, that the Romans built along the Rhine and Danube rivers in around 100 AD. When Hofstede interviewed IBM employees from various countries in the 1960s, he came across this cultural divide without looking for it. Given the clear differences Hofstede found in the scores for power distance in the northern and southern European countries and the fact that this divide has been in existence for so long, it is fair to conclude that the differences between the north and the south of the continent are structural. Before expanding on the challenges this implies for the European integration project let us examine the consequences of this cultural divide.

Consequences of Cultural Differences

We have already seen that participants from Germanic countries will invest more tokens in a joint project than those from Latin countries. The same studies show that this behaviour increases the average return. Without the possibility to punish free-riders the returns in

---

41 Ibid., p. 262.

such public good games were around 10 per cent higher in northern Europe than in southern countries, with returns almost 50 per cent higher where the possibility to punish was included.[42]

Table 4.3 shows that this result applies not only to games but also to real life. In the year 1500, the size of the economy of the (five) Latin countries was double that of the (eight) Germanic ones. By 1820, after the Napoleonic wars, the economies of the two blocs were roughly the same size. The more rapid growth of the Germanic bloc has continued ever since with its economy now being significantly larger than that of the Latin bloc. It is likely that this catch-up started earlier but this cannot be demonstrated in figures owing to the lack of reliable data. However, if we look at the economic performance of the two cultural groups from the perspective of population size, we can go right back to the start of our era. Around the start of the first millennium the population of the five Latin countries – then part of the Roman Empire – was more than three times larger than that of the Germanic bloc (17 million versus 5 million). A thousand years on, this lead had shrunk to double the number and by the year 2000 the population of the Latin countries was actually smaller than that of the Germanic ones.[43]

Table 4.3 Size of the economy

Year	Latin Europe	Germanic Europe	Difference
1500	28.0	14.2	13.8
1600	38.5	24.3	14.2
1700	44.1	33.3	10.8
1820	74.8	77.1	−2.3
1900	223.8	407.2	−183.4
2000	3,196.9	3,710.4	−513.5

Source: Maddison (2003), table 1b, Gross Domestic Product (in 1990 international Geary-Khamis dollars × bln) of the same five/eight countries as in the previous tables.

---

42 Herrmann, Thöni and Gächter (2008), Supporting Material 2.3; Masclet and Villeval (2008), table 5. This data is not included in the sources for Spain and Italy cited in chapter III.1.

43 Maddison (2003), table 8a. The eight Germanic countries took longer to overtake the five Latin nations in terms of population (around 1880) than in terms of their economy (around 1820).

Differences in national behaviour, both in an economic sense and otherwise, are the result of cultural differences. How did the cultural characteristics of a certain society evolve and why did the process happen in the way it did? Can the origins of the high scores for the basic value of power distance in southern Europe be traced back to the Roman Empire? Perhaps these scores originated during Rome's early history, when the new city state had to defend itself against rivals from Latium and Etruria and was forced to attract large numbers of immigrants in order to form armies. The leaders of the various Roman clans, the patres familias, sought to secure their position against threat from the incomers by establishing a sizeable distance between themselves and the newcomers. Perhaps this military discipline then filtered through into family life, resulting in wives and children having a deep and permanent sense of fear for their lord and master, in the same way as soldiers for their officers and clients for their patrons. Severe punishments awaited anyone who failed in this strict obedience. The permanent need to consider a strict authority may have resulted in a value system characterised by a large power distance.

We can also imagine the establishment of a very different value system among the Germanic peoples living in their villages by the Baltic Sea in the centuries before the beginning of our era. The low score for power distance could, for example, be the result of the need for members of the tribe to adapt to the natural environment they lived in. Perhaps they needed to build dykes to prevent settlements from being washed away during storms. Such work can only be done in collaboration, with the same applying to the maintenance work after the storm has passed. In order to survive, all villagers constantly had to engage in such joint projects, meaning that the notion that 'we are all equal' gradually became part of daily life and was subconsciously passed on to new generations.

Besides functional adaptation to external threats from enemies or nature, certain scores for power distance among some peoples can also be due to coincidence. Dutch biologist Frans de Waal gives an example from the animal world based on his study of two large groups of giant apes at the Wisconsin Primate Center.

When I worked there, I could see, side by side, one group in which males fiercely competed every mating season and another group in which they did not. In the first group, the alpha male would not allow any other male in his sight to mount a female. This didn't stop the other males from mating; they seized every opportunity when the old leader had his back turned. Other high-ranking males were equally intolerant, however, prohibiting matings by males below them. In the other group, five adult males might each be consorting with a female in plain view of the others without any interference. Of course, the alpha male had first pick, but he tolerated the others' sexual activity. Both groups had many more females than males, so the difference cannot be attributed to the relative availability of females. I studied these groups for a decade, and the contrasting male relations persisted despite changes in the hierarchy.[44]

In this instance, the difference in power distance between the two groups was a matter of chance, caused by the different characters of the two leaders. In the first group, the other males were afraid of being caught by the leader and craftily went behind his back. The atmosphere in the second group was very different: naturally the boss had first pick but otherwise the other members of the group were free to do as they pleased. Could it be that the leaders of early Rome just happened to be autocratic by nature and that their relentless severity was passed down to subsequent generations? And could it be that the early chiefs of Germanic tribes were more similar to the alpha male in the second group, meaning that members of the group are not afraid to do their own thing?

We don't know. It would seem obvious to assume that the origins of all kinds of group characteristics lie in a distant past and over the centuries have been passed down from generation to generation. Any rational adaptations to the circumstances that applied back then have long since lost their relevance; modern Romans no longer need to defend themselves against attacks from neighbouring cities, any more than the modern Dutch and Germans need to grab spades to protect themselves from high tides. We are not aware of our basic values but they still have implications for the way we feel and, therefore, act.

---

44 Waal (2001), p. 204.

What happened next with the Ancient Germans and Romans? The Germanic tribes started moving south from their early settlements on the shores of the Baltic Sea and the Romans moved north from what is now Italy. From the first century BC, when their paths met they were at war. From 12 BC to 16 AD the Romans attempted to conquer Germania and make the River Elbe the border of the empire. In spite of their military superiority their attempts failed. Roman generals including Drusus, Tiberius and Germanicus advanced through the entire region and reached the Elbe on several occasions. But during these campaigns the Roman legions found no cities that they could conquer or occupy, but instead only small, abandoned villages that were easy for their inhabitants to rebuild after the Romans had moved on. The Romans were unable to occupy the region permanently. In the end Emperor Tiberius decided around 100 AD to abandon the conquest of Germania. A permanent border was established along the Rhine and the Danube, consisting of military fortifications with a connecting road running parallel to the two rivers. The fortifications varied in size from large and smaller fortresses to simple watchtowers. The Romans and the peoples they had conquered lived to the west and south of this border with the 'barbarians' on the other side. This military zone, the *limes*, existed for around four hundred years and played a major role in the establishment of the cultural borders in Western Europe.

Despite their technological, organisational and military superiority the Romans ultimately lost this confrontation. On the night of 31 December 405 AD, a mixed group of Germanic tribes including Vandals and Alans crossed the Rhine and did not return to their own lands. They started roaming around the Roman Empire and were followed by other tribes. Unable to defeat them the Romans could only look on as the Germanic tribes advanced as far as North Africa in the fifth century AD and eventually sacked the city of Rome.

Were these Germanic successes the unavoidable consequence of the 'iron rule' that groups which are dominated by cooperators will ultimately be stronger than groups in which self-seeking individuals are more prominent? Did the freedom and honesty of the Germanic group ultimately trump Latin obedience and organisation? We have tracked these differences through the centuries, contrasting Germanic dice-players with Martial's clients, Imma with Benedict,

Chaucer with Boccaccio, the Austrian emperors with Louis XIV, Schacht with Poincaré, right through to Wulff and Berlusconi in our own times. After some 2,000 years, the descendants of the Ancient Germans have succeeded in turning their original economic disadvantage compared to the Latin peoples into a lead.

The difference in performance between the two blocs is not confined to Europe. We can see it if we compare the United States, which belongs to the Germanic cultural bloc, to the Latin sphere of South and Central America. In the period between 1500 and 1700 AD the North American economy was only one-tenth of the size of that of South America. Today the United States economy is more than two-and-a-half times the size of that of its southern neighbours.

Successful States

In their book *Why Nations Fail* US economists Daron Acemoglu and James Robinson employ different terminology to explain why some countries are more successful than others.[45] They distinguish countries according to the presence of inclusive or extractive institutions. In the political sphere the dominance of inclusive institutions means that the power resides with many groups within the population. This pluralistic model contrasts with the absolutist variant, in which power is unlimited and is held by a small group. In the economic sphere, inclusive institutions encourage a majority of the population to participate in economic activities by developing their talents and applying these as they see fit. In such a society the judicial system will be honest, all citizens will have equal access to public services, and property rights and new entrants to various markets will be protected. By contrast, extractive economic institutions are aimed at protecting the income and wealth of the top layer of the population against potential competitors.

The dynamics in both types of society are characterised by virtuous and vicious circles. In a virtuous circle, successful newcomers such as business people or politicians will make every effort to prevent old rulers from regaining their position. This is because the newcomers are not sure they will be able to displace the old guard

---

45 Acemoglu and Robinson (2012).

another time. This is why pluralism, once established, will tend to evolve. This gives more and more people a chance of advancement, for example, because they are better educated and better informed by the media about various societal developments.

A vicious circle also has the tendency to perpetuate itself. Exploitative political and economic bodies reinforce one another, for example, by preventing controls on abuse of power. The penalty for loss of position is so great for the ruling oligarchy – as is the reward for maintaining it – that they will do everything they can to resist any threat from new entrants.

We have already seen that self-seeking free-riders play a more important role in society in the Latin countries than in the Germanic nations, where the cooperators are dominant. These latter nations are also those which are characterised by inclusive institutions and virtuous circles. By contrast, in the Latin countries we are more likely to encounter extractive institutions that create and perpetuate vicious circles.

Is it possible to identify any particular moments in the history of the Latin countries when an exceptional combination of circumstances meant that there was an opportunity to break the vicious circle?

In France such an opportunity presented itself just after the Second World War. It was the time of the Fourth Republic, established in 1946 under a coalition government of three parties which had been active in the resistance against the German oppressors: the Socialists, the Communists and the Popular Republican Movement (MRP), a new Christian-Democrat party which advocated fundamental reform of French society. The party put the public interest first and sought to end the clientelistic practices of the pre-war era. This idealism was not understood by everyone; even members of parliament for the MRP complained that their ministers treated them the same as delegates of other parties. 'Many deputies do not obtain what they demand from an MRP Minister. In the other parties the organization of services rendered works fully. But in order to see an MRP Minister, it is better to go by way of the intervention of a deputy of another [political] tendency.'[46]

In *Maigret and the Minister*, Simenon describes how this unique phase in French politics unfolded. A minister under pressure expresses his

---

46 Warner (2001), pp. 140–41.

feelings to the chief inspector. 'A brand-new parliament, you'll probably recall, when we had sworn there'd be no more shady goings-on.
It was immediately after the war and the country was riding on a
wave of idealism. People wanted integrity.' But it didn't last for long.

> We are together every day, we shake hands like old friends. By
> the time parliament's been in session for a few weeks, everyone's
> on first-name terms and politicians do one another small
> favours. Each day you shake more hands and if those hands
> aren't very clean, you shrug indulgently. 'Well! He's not a bad
> fellow.' Or else: 'He has to do that to keep his voters happy.'[47]

The MRP did not last long. Altruistic cooperators who put the
common interest above their own are doomed to fail in an environment dominated by self-seeking free-riders. After 20 administrations
in 12 years and despite all the good intentions to break with the past,
the Fourth Republic finally collapsed in 1958.

For Spain, the moment of truth came in 1975 with the death of
General Franco. During his almost 40 years in power the dictator had
pursued a policy of economic self-sufficiency. This policy meant that
people with the right contacts were able to obtain licences to import
certain essential goods and sell them on at high profits, thus accumu-
lating vast fortunes. But now everything was going to change! Pepe
Carvalho, our private detective from Barcelona, knows all about this.
He is no longer getting assignments to track down runaway wives and
daughters because their husbands and fathers no longer care. 'The
basic values have been lost. You people wanted democracy, didn't
you?' Pepe is not the only one with problems. 'Doctors and notaries
were also victims of democracy. They had to pay their taxes now and
they were beginning to think that perhaps it was preferable to have
been professionals living under fascism while practicing a degree of
liberal resistance.'[48]

In another book, a senior civil servant describes to Pepe Carvalho
how Franco's ruling and wealthy class managed to survive the transi-
tion to democratic rule.

---

47 Simenon (2017), pp. 102, 104.
48 Vázquez Montalbán (2012), pp. 7–8.

I know about the Gausachs family from when we were doing a study of Catalonia's economy. The name came up, and since it turns out that one of the Gausachs is tied up with the far Left I was curious to find out about the rest of the family. They've got all sorts. A Maoist, and another one who's more or less a Maoist. Then there's Martin, the perfect executive. Another brother supports the nationalists. He's got a daughter who's in the Communist Party, and two young boys still at college – one studying with the Opus, and the other with the Jesuits.[49]

In these uncertain times the Gausachs family are unable to assess how the channels of power will run in the future and so they make sure to keep as many options open as they can: some members of the family are active with political parties on the (extreme) left and right, while others maintain ties with the church and the business sector. Only just recently Pablo Iglesias, the leader of the political party Podemos, referred to 'these families whose surnames we still all know' to underline that families such as these came through the regime change successfully. In Spain, too, it would seem that the oligarchy is reluctant to surrender its position. In neither France nor Spain did altruistic cooperators manage to use the post-war years to break the spiral of exploitation of the majority of the population by a small elite.

Latin-Germanic Cooperation

People cooperate better when they trust each other. This applies both nationally and internationally. Table 4.4 shows that European managers have a clear opinion about the trustworthiness of their colleagues in various neighbouring countries.

It's a familiar picture. Almost everyone finds Germans the most trustworthy. Along with the Brits they form the Germanic contingent in this study. All the managers surveyed, including those from southern Europe, considered colleagues from these countries to be the most trustworthy. The Italians are the least trustworthy; they themselves agree, albeit that they rank the Spaniards even lower.

---

49 Ibid., p. 74.

Table 4.4 Trust in European managers (1 = most, 4 = least)

Countries	Germany	United Kingdom	Spain	Italy
GERMAN VIEW	1	2	3	4
UK VIEW	2	1	3	4
SPANISH VIEW	1	2	3	4
ITALIAN VIEW	1	2	4	3

Source: Guiso, Sapienza and Zingales (2005). Study by 3i/Cranfield European Enterprise Centre.

Comparisons between levels of trust and trustworthiness among northern and southern Europeans have also been made in a study involving a public good game whereby 'senders' from the two regions transfer tokens to 'receivers' over several rounds of the game.[50] The greater the number of tokens transferred, the greater the level of trust. The trustworthiness of the players is measured by the number of tokens that the receivers then return to the senders. Senders and receivers from both groups are free in their choice of the number of tokens they return and in their choice of counterparties.

The study showed that in the first round of the game northern and southern Europeans send each other roughly the same number of tokens. But subsequently it transpires that the southern Europeans have a lower propensity to reciprocate than their northern counterparts. As a result, in subsequent rounds northern Europeans show a preference for players from their own cultural group. Given that this discrimination of the southern Europeans is not compensated by their own group, they lag further and further behind as the game progresses. By the end of the game it is the northern Europeans who have both sent and received the largest number of tokens. The southern Europeans are less successful because of the lower level of trust they have in each other. This result echoes the survey among

---

50 Bornhorst, Ichino, Schlag and Winter (2004). In this study, 'Southern Europe' comprises the same five countries that I use. 'Northern Europe' is supplemented with Poland, Belgium and Finland while Norway is not included. Overall there is an 83 per cent overlap between the northern European participants in this study and my classification.

managers in which Italians and Spaniards also consider their fellow professionals in Germany and the United Kingdom to be more trustworthy than colleagues from their own country.

Studies have also been carried out into cooperation between participants from individual countries. One study into the behaviour of Brits and Italians in another public good game showed that the Brits, as expected, invested more (9 per cent) in the joint project than the Italians.[51] If the game is subsequently played in mixed groups it transpires that the investments are lower compared to games involving only Brits (20 per cent lower) or only Italians (11 per cent lower). This shows that the better the understanding between the members of the group the greater the willingness to cooperate. Being a member of the same cultural group – be that Latin or Germanic or a certain nationality – helps in this respect.

Situations like this are very familiar to me. For years I took part in international investment meetings. Representatives of banks and securities brokers from various countries would meet to discuss the expected developments in exchange rates, interest rates and share prices. Apart from the differences in behaviour in the actual meeting (the Dutch seek consensus, the French want to shine), during breaks the party would without fail separate into the same two groups: the Dutch would drink coffee with the Brits and the Germans, while the French, Spaniards and Italians would spontaneously form into another group. The two cultural groups were clearly discernible in the meeting room.

When engaging in international projects it is therefore wise to bear in mind these communication pitfalls which do not occur at national level. The Eurovision Song Contest provides a rich source of examples of this problem. Eurovision, which has been going for almost as long as the European Union and its predecessors, is a singing contest in which almost all the European countries compete for the title. Every year the excitement reaches fever pitch when the voting starts, with the countries awarding each other points for each song, and every year there are accusations of favouritism. For the fans it's a familiar story. Let's take the Scandinavian bloc. Since televoting by the viewers was introduced in 1998, Norway has awarded Sweden

---

51 Castro (2008).

an average of 7.8 votes and the Swedes their neighbours an average of 7.2. These scores are considerably higher than the average of 5.5 that countries should award each other based on the point system used. The Netherlands and Belgium also favour one another, with the Dutch awarding the Belgians an average of 6.7 votes and the Belgians repaying this more than generously by awarding the Dutch an average of 9.0 votes.

But out of the more than 40 countries that take part there is one pair of countries that easily beat all the other friendly combinations: Greece and its Greek-speaking neighbour Cyprus always award each other the maximum 12 points. It would seem that neither the members of the jury nor the people using the televoting system in Greece and Cyprus have any scruples about showing other participants that they are prepared to completely disregard the whole point of the contest: to pick the best song. Friends support each other through thick and thin, and all other considerations are irrelevant.

The behaviour of the Greek representatives at Eurovision can at times also be rather egocentric. For example, after the first rehearsals in Birmingham in 1998 the Greek composer Yannis Valvis was unhappy with the way the BBC intended to film his song and asked for the Greeks to be given full control over the performance of Greek entry. Given that no country enjoys such a privilege, his request was rejected. Unwilling to leave things at that, the composer used the Greek press conference to launch a formal protest. This left the organisers, the European Broadcasting Union and the BBC, with no option but to refuse Valvis entry to the arena on finals day, after which the Hellenic Broadcasting Corporation threatened to withdraw from the contest. Having realised that this would not achieve anything, they then swiftly changed their mind again. However, the Greeks had overplayed their hand; their song was awarded not a single vote – apart, of course, from the 12 points from Cyprus.[52]

Cooperation is an art in the best of circumstances and is certainly a difficult task at an international level. That cooperation between so many European countries after the Second World War ever progressed to the stage where integration could be considered is an exceptional achievement for that reason alone. The question

---

52 http://en.wikipedia.org/wiki/Eurovision-Song-Contest-1998.

that now remains is: where do we go from here? Is it possible for us to pursue further integration while recognising the consequences of cultural differences? Or, will we go on pretending that all countries are equal and share the same wishes with regard to implementing the commonly agreed policies?

Chapter 5

THE EUROPEAN UNION TODAY

The graph shows a sharp fall in the European Union's popularity across Western Europe in recent years. In most countries, both in the Latin south and the Germanic north, the percentage of the population that feels positive towards the Union fell from around 50 per cent (in 2005) to around 30 per cent (in 2016). This means that in most countries the level is now similar to that in Eurosceptic nations such as the United Kingdom, Austria and Sweden. A month after the compilation of the 2016 Eurobarometer shown in Figure 5.1, a majority of UK voters voted in favour of Brexit. Does this mean that countries such as Germany, Spain and Greece, where the EU is even less popular than in the United Kingdom, might also want to leave the EU?

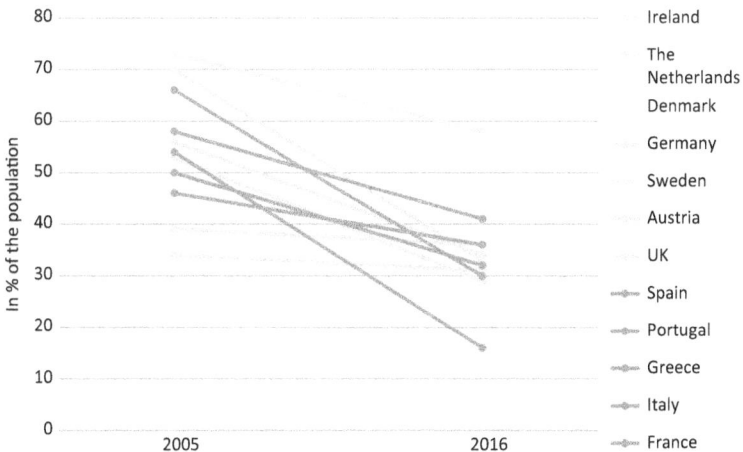

Figure 5.1 Positive perception of the European Union.

Source: Eurobarometer.

While things are not quite that straightforward, it is clear that the EU is in choppy waters. Can the tide still be turned or are the Eurosceptics set to gain the upper hand in more countries? In this chapter I will look at what a majority of the population feel that the EU is doing well and what not, and what changes could improve the Union's chances of survival. I will also examine how the proposed changes could be implemented. It is important to bear in mind in this context that in a democracy it is ultimately the people who decide, not the politicians and not the experts they rely on.

Stronger Together

Solar Panels from China

EU ProSun is the organisation that represents the interests of a majority of EU manufacturers of solar panels. On 25 July 2012, the lobby group filed an anti-dumping complaint with the European Commission against their Chinese competitors. According to EU ProSun figures, global consumption of solar panels in 2011 equalled 28 gigawatts (GW) while Chinese production capacity equalled 45 GW. With Chinese domestic demand equalling just 2 GW, the rest of the output was exported – predominantly to the EU (22 GW) at prices that were more than 80 per cent lower than in 2008.[1] If this was allowed to continue, European manufacturers would be pushed out and China would control the global market.

EU ProSun argued its case by pointing out that thanks to high automation, labour accounted for only 10 per cent of production costs in the EU, making European manufacturers globally competitive. China, a cheap labour country, had no cost advantage over European producers resulting from lower wages as these were offset by higher transport costs. China, however, did benefit from massive subsidies in the form of cheap loans from state-controlled banks and low prices for energy and business premises. EU ProSun therefore called on the EU to impose anti-dumping duties to offset these subsidies.

---

1 EU ProSun Fact Sheet (www.prosun.org/en/fact-sheet-en/).

The request found fertile soil. European Commissioner for Trade Karel de Gucht had long been irked by these unfair Chinese trade practices. In a speech on EU–Chinese trade relations in London some two weeks before EU ProSun filed its complaint, he said: 'We should express ourselves where we have concerns about specific Chinese policies. For instance, the role of state-owned enterprises and subsidisation at the core of the Chinese economy is something we are looking at very closely. We have also been very clear with our Chinese counterparts that we do not appreciate their use of threats and intimidation towards our companies behind the scenes.'[2]

De Gucht made swift work of launching an investigation into the cut-price Chinese solar panels and some months later 'the European Commission concluded that the fair value of a Chinese solar panel sold in Europe should be 88 per cent higher than the price at which it is sold. Thus, from August 2013, the duty on Chinese exports was increased from an initial 11.8 per cent to 47.6 per cent.'[3]

Unfortunately, the trade commissioner is only authorised to impose temporary duties; definitive implementation requires approval by the member states. To De Gucht's frustration this was not forthcoming. After a visit by the Chinese Prime Minister Li Keqiang to Chancellor Merkel it became clear that Germany would vote against because of Chinese threats to impose import duties on luxury cars. France and the other southern European countries also left the trade commissioner in the lurch after China announced its intention to launch an investigation into European wine imports. In the end, 18 of the 27 EU member states voted against De Gucht's plans and he was forced to seek another solution. The compromise, applicable from July 2013 to end-2015, set a minimum price of 0.56 euro for every watt produced by Chinese solar panels. EU ProSun, which had called for a price of 0.80 euro, said, 'This agreement is not a solution but a capitulation.' In addition, it was agreed that Chinese products sold below the minimum price would be subject to anti-dumping duties of up to 47 per cent.[4]

---

2 Gucht (2012).
3 Yu Chen (2015).
4 *Financial Times*, 31 July 2013.

In December 2015, the European Commission announced that the measures against the dumping of Chinese solar panels would be extended. EU ProSun welcomed this step and stated that the policy had brought the market share of the Chinese down from over 80 per cent. 'More than half of the European production capacity for solar cells and modules has been preserved, and manufacturers are investing millions of euros in new solar production and research in Europe. In 2016 alone well over 100 Million Euro investments are planned.'[5] The result did please the European manufacturers. A survey of solar installation companies across the EU showed that 88 per cent of installers considered it important or very important that products from Europe and countries of origin other than China were available in the EU market.[6]

Although trade commissioner De Gucht was initially disappointed that so many member states had capitulated to Chinese threats, the final result proved to be not unsatisfactory. Certainly the European industry was satisfied, and judging by the investment plans was looking to the future with optimism. By taking joint action against a trading partner that was more powerful than the individual member states the EU had managed to preserve an important branch of industry. How will the United Kingdom deal with a situation like this in the future when it has to tackle such negotiations on its own?

The cultural gap between northern and southern Europe was not in evidence during these negotiations; all member states benefited from the joint action. However, a study into restrictive import measures from 1991 to 2003 shows that the two cultural regions are usually discernible. On 85 per cent occasions or more, the five Latin countries had supported steps towards anti-dumping duties while the Germanic member states had done so less than 15 per cent of the time.[7] It would therefore seem that the cultural divide within the EU does play a role in international trade policy even if this was not apparent in the battle concerning the solar panels.

---

5 EU ProSun press release, 5 December 2015.

6 *EU Reporter*, 19 August 2016.

7 Evenett and Vermulst (2005). Belgium, Austria and Ireland constitute an inter-
   mediate group which traded their votes for other concessions.

Trucks on the Internal Market

The European Commission does not only have a mandate to negotiate on behalf of the member states with other countries such as China but is also responsible for monitoring the European internal market. Since import duties between the member states were abolished the EU has formed a single marketplace where companies are free to engage in cross-border trade. To ensure fair competition product standards (ranging from food safety to power sockets) need to be harmonised and monopolies and cartels must be prevented. A cartel is when companies in a certain industry reach mutual agreements as a result of which consumers pay more than they would in the event of free competition.

Each year the European competition commissioner brings action against between 10 and 50 cartels in a wide range of economic sectors. The biggest fish caught to date was announced on 19 July 2016 by the Danish commissioner Margrethe Vestager.

> We have today put down a marker by imposing record fines for a serious infringement. In all, there are over 30 million trucks on European roads, which account for around three quarters of inland transport of goods in Europe and play a vital role for the European economy. It is not acceptable that MAN, Volvo/ Renault, Daimler, Iveco and DAF, which together account for around 9 out of every 10 medium and heavy trucks produced in Europe, were part of a cartel instead of competing with each other. For 14 years they colluded on the pricing and on passing on the costs for meeting environmental standards to customers. This is also a clear message to companies that cartels are not accepted.[8]

What led up to this triumphant announcement? The Commission received a tip-off, probably in the course of 2010, from within the German MAN group regarding the existence of a cartel. A year later the Commission announced it had started to undertake unannounced inspections at the premises of companies active in the truck industry

---

8 European Commission press release, 19 July 2016.

in several member states as 'a preliminary step into suspected anticompetitive practices'.[9]

The investigation revealed that from 1997 to 2004 senior managers had met on the sidelines of trade fairs and other events. From 2004 the organisation was done via the German subsidiaries of the participating companies with communications taking place via email. The agreements concerned the factory gate prices of trucks, the timing of the introduction of new emission technologies and the charging on of costs to customers.

The Commission operates a leniency policy for this type of situation under which the cartel member that initially informs the Commission of the existence of the cartel is exempt from prosecution and immune from any resulting fine. The cartel member then admits its guilt and is most cooperative receives a 50 per cent discount on the fine imposed and so on. The policy is extremely successful and most cartel investigations are now instigated under the leniency policy. This prompts a 'race to confess' among the cartel members.

This also happened in the case of the truck cartel. MAN was the whistleblower and thus avoided a fine of around 1.2 billion euros. Volvo/Renault was the second most skilful at the game and only had to pay half (670 million euros). DAF of the Netherlands received a mere 10 per cent discount (and paid 753 million euros).[10] The total financial damage to the sector to date amounts to 2.9 billion euros, more than double the previous record.[11]

It goes without saying that the reputational damage to those companies which are exposed is part of the punishment. Volvo president and CEO Martin Lundstedt took it on the chin. 'We strive to be a world leading business because we compete with the best products [...] While we regret what has happened, we are convinced that these events have not impacted our customers. The Volvo Group has always competed for every single transaction.'[12]

---

9 European Commission press release, 18 January 2011.

10 Swedish company Scania rejected the Commission's offer and will pursue its case in the courts in the coming years.

11 In 2012, a number of manufacturers of TV and computer monitor tubes, including the Dutch company Philips, were fined a combined total of 1.4 billion euros.

12 *EU Reporter*, 19 July 2016.

It is an optimistic assessment. If Volvo and its cartel partners fail to reach an agreement with their duped customers the latter will surely brush such fine words aside and take them to court to recoup the damages.

Commissioner Vestager does not focus solely on European companies that break the competition rules and disadvantage their clients. Investigations were also launched against Gazprom of Russia (that was accused of charging some Eastern European countries up to 40 per cent more for gas than other buyers; this case was settled in May 2018 without a fine) and US group Google (that was charged with abuse of its dominant position by requiring mobile phone manufacturers to pre-install its apps on devices using its Android operating system; in July 2018, the EU imposed a 4.34-billion euro fine on the US giant – a new record).

Because of the economic weight it represents, the European Commission is more capable of taking on such global players than individual European states. EU citizens benefit from this but pay little attention to the positive role of the EU. The procedures are so lengthy and so complicated that few people are able to keep up with the key aspects of such confrontations.

In the example of the truck cartel there is no clear difference in behaviour between the Germanic and Latin countries. Clients and competitors in all member states benefit from the intervention. Might the cultural divide have played a role if the home countries of the six manufacturers had been less widely distributed across the EU? In the case in question the home bases of the offenders ranged from the deep south (Iveco of Italy) to the high north (Scania and Volvo of Sweden). How might the process have gone if, for example, five of the six companies involved had been German or Spanish? Would these countries have resisted the high fines or would they have accepted the European legal process? Other sectors, for example, energy providers, enjoy more political protection in the Latin countries than in the Germanic ones. Here the cultural divide is clearly visible and the internal market works differently in the north and the south of the continent. This does not, however, alter the fact that European consumers benefit from joint action taken against globally operating companies, whether they be European or from other continents.

A Step Back

As we have seen, the EU plays an important role in trade, both between the member states and with external parties. United we stand. In addition to free movement of goods and services the EU also provides for free movement of people and capital. These elements of the Union are more controversial. First I will discuss the functioning of the common labour market. Then we will examine the asylum policy for non-EU migrants. Finally we will take a look at the functioning of the European Central Bank (ECB).

A Single European Labour Market

In 2004, eight former communist Eastern European countries joined the European Union (Figure 5.2). The same year saw the EU directive on the free movement of people come into force. This gives all EU citizens, whether they are in work or not, the right to settle in any member state, where they are entitled to the same social security provisions

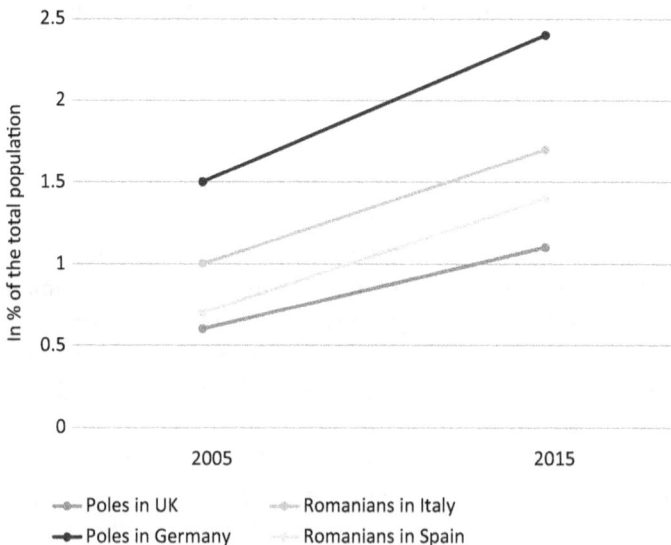

Figure 5.2 Internal EU migration, 2005–15.

Source: United Nations, Trends in international migrant stock: Migrants by destination and origin, 2015; own calculations.

(such as unemployment benefits, income support, old-age pension and occupational disability payments) as citizens of the host nation.

Given that both wages and benefits are considerably higher in the old EU countries than in Eastern Europe, it is no surprise that this resulted in a massive wave of migrants from east to west. The graph shows that in 2005 Poles accounted for 0.6 per cent of the total UK population. By 2015 this had risen to 1.1 per cent (an increase from 329,000 to 703,000 individuals). The figures for Germany are almost double. Romanians are mainly attracted to Italy and Spain.

Many longer-standing EU members agreed a transitional regime setting a cap on the number of immigrants in the first few years. Certain others, including the United Kingdom, considered such curbs to be unnecessary. This proved to be a miscalculation: the British open-door policy resulted in 600,000 migrant workers arriving in the space of two years compared to an expected number of 30,000. It therefore came as no surprise when in 2006 the UK government did set limits for the number of migrants from Romania and Bulgaria with those countries set to join the EU the following year. Home Secretary John Reid acknowledged that some schools had had to cope with a significant rise in pupils, while some councils had reported overcrowding in private housing.[13]

The tensions between the Brits and the immigrant workers have persisted ever since. In 2011, only 19 per cent of the population believed that immigration had a positive effect on their country with 62 per cent believing that immigrants made it harder for them to find a job. While this attitude softened somewhat over the next few years, the improvement was insufficient to prevent a majority of voters from voting in favour of leaving the EU in the referendum of 23 June 2016.[14] While there were obviously a great many other arguments that contributed to this outcome, most polls conducted shortly before the referendum date showed that immigration, which in the eyes of

---

13 BBC News, 24 October 2006.
14 IPSOS, Global Views on Immigration and the Refugee Crisis (2016). This survey conducted in 23 countries relates to both asylum seekers and economic migrants. Given that the United Kingdom took in virtually no asylum seekers during these years, I assume that the British responses should be viewed mainly as a reaction to migrants from Eastern Europe.

the UK population was dominated by Eastern Europeans, was the main reason for this result.[15]

Voters in the referendum took little notice of the many studies by influential institutions such as the IMF, OECD, Bank of England and University College London (UCL), which all pointed to Brexit having a considerable negative impact on the British economy and jobs. Professor Christian Dustmann, co-author of the UCL study, said: 'A key concern of the public debate on migration is whether immigrants contribute their fair share to the tax and welfare systems. Our new analysis draws a positive picture of the overall fiscal contribution made by recent immigrant cohorts, particularly of immigrants arriving from the EU.'[16]

This is very different language to that used by *The Sun* a few days before the referendum. The tabloid reported on an advertisement from project developer AA Homes and Housing which read: 'A big construction company in South London is looking for Polish kitchen fitters, plumbers, tilers, carpenters and labourers.' Scaffolder Josh Turvey, 26, from Camden, North London, was 'disgusted' when he saw it online and called it discrimination against British workers. He added: 'We're losing out on work and being undercut all the time because firms know they can employ Eastern Europeans on the cheap [...] Foreign workers will just keep undercutting us which is why I and 99 per cent of British construction workers want out of Europe.'[17] Other newspapers also carried stories about contractors suddenly wanting language skills, with Polish, Romanian and Bulgarian in particular being in demand.

Labourers were not the only people to vote for Brexit. Marina Lewycka, a moderate left-wing university lecturer, wrote a best-selling novel based on her own family history. Her Ukrainian parents came to England in 1947. In *A Short History of Tractors in Ukrainian* she tells

---

15 For example, the IPSOS MORI poll for the week of 11–14 June 2016: 33 per cent of respondents cited the number of immigrants coming into Britain as being the most important issue in deciding which way to vote in the referendum, making this the top response. Only 6 per cent of respondents cited Britain's ability to trade with EU countries as the most important issue in the referendum.

16 *The Guardian*, 5 November 2014.

17 *The Sun*, 17 June 2016.

the story of her elderly father of 84 who wants to save a 36-year-old divorcee from his home country. His daughter, who shares all the characteristics of the author, is listening to her father.

> He has known her for three months [...] She wants to make a new life for herself and her son in the West, a good life, with good job, good money, nice car – absolutely no Lada no Skoda – good education for son – must be Oxford Cambridge, nothing less [...] She sits on his lap and allows him to fondle her breasts. They are happy together.
>
> 'Oh, well [...]' I keep my voice steady, but rage burns in my heart, 'life's just full of surprises. [...] But, look, Pappa [...] I can see why you want to marry her. But have you asked yourself why she wants to marry *you*?'
>
> '*Tak tak*. Yes, yes, I know. Passport. Visa. Work permit. So vat?'

The lady in question, named Valentina, lives up to all the prejudices. She fleeces the old man for all he's worth and turns against him once he's broke. 'You no good man. You plenty-money meanie. Promise money. Money sit in bank. Promise car. Crap car.'

A few months later, after her father has been constantly terrorised and swindled, the daughter's ideals lie in ruins. 'I used to be liberal about immigration – I suppose I just thought it was all right for people to live where they wanted. But now I imagine hordes of Valentinas barging their way through customs, at Ramsgate, at Felixstowe, at Dover, at Newhaven – pouring off the boats, purposeful, single-minded, mad.'[18]

The wide-spread discontent with the arrival of so many Eastern Europeans, who mainly present a threat to low-skilled workers in the labour market, was not limited to the United Kingdom. In countries including the Netherlands, France and Sweden incumbent governments watched in fear as anti-immigrant parties grew in strength. They succeeded in getting the European Commission to propose a revision of the EU Posted Workers Directive. Under this guideline employees who work temporarily in another EU country

---

18 Lewycka (2006), pp. 2, 87, 160.

are entitled to receive at least the minimum rate of pay applicable in the host country. Social security contributions are, however, paid in the home country. Because these contributions tend to be lower over there, Eastern European workers are still cheaper. Under the slogan 'equal pay for equal work' the Commission sought to end this discrepancy.

The Eastern European member states were radically opposed, fearing that their compatriots would no longer be able to find work in the west. The French Prime Minister Manuel Valls in particular, under pressure from the Front National, expressed outrage at this opposition. 'If it is not possible to convince [the EU to change the law] France will not apply this directive.'[19] In the Netherlands it was mainly the minister of Social Affairs Lodewijk Asscher who was vocal on the subject. 'The number of secondments is rising very sharply [...] Particularly in sectors with insecure work contracts, low-skilled workers, people with a migrant background [...] If you don't solve this, you are letting down a group of people who have little scope for resolving things for themselves.'[20]

It looked as if the combination of a large number of Eastern European countries joining the EU and the further expansion of the free movement of people in 2004 had been too much of a good thing. A large section of the population of the old member states felt threatened by the large numbers of immigrants on the job market and was angry about benefits that the newcomers were entitled to if they became unemployed or sick. The EU was blamed for these woes. To avoid further erosion of popular support for the Union in the coming years I believe that there is no option but to take measures to slow down further integration of the European labour market. Understandably, the Eastern Europeans will resent this but they will also be keen to avoid any more Brexits. Because that would risk the doors to many more Western European countries being slammed shut.

There is no cultural divide in evidence here: both the northern and the southern member states are seeking the same kind of measures under pressure from large sections of their populations. What is

---

19 *NRC Handelsblad*, 18 July 2016.

20 Ibid., 20 April 2016.

striking is that, as the graph shows, Romanians – who speak a Latin-based language – have such a strong preference for Italy and Spain. Poles prefer the Germanic countries.

Asylum Seekers

The number of asylum seekers seeking refuge in the EU has been rising for years, but the number suddenly spiked in 2014/15, with the civil wars in Syria, Afghanistan and Iraq in particular creating huge refugee flows (Figure 5.3). Over the two years, Germany took in 4.2 asylum seekers per 1,000 inhabitants. Sweden topped the list with over 12 asylum seekers per 1,000 inhabitants. Portugal and Spain made virtually no contribution towards solving this crisis; during these years the southern European countries took in only 0.7 asylum seeker per 1,000 inhabitants compared to 5.5 for the northern European countries.[21] The Germanic-Latin cultural divide is in clear evidence here.

How can this be so? After all, hadn't most refugees reached the EU via Greece and Italy? Under EU law, the country that played the greatest part in an asylum seeker's entry to or stay on EU territory is responsible for dealing with their asylum application.

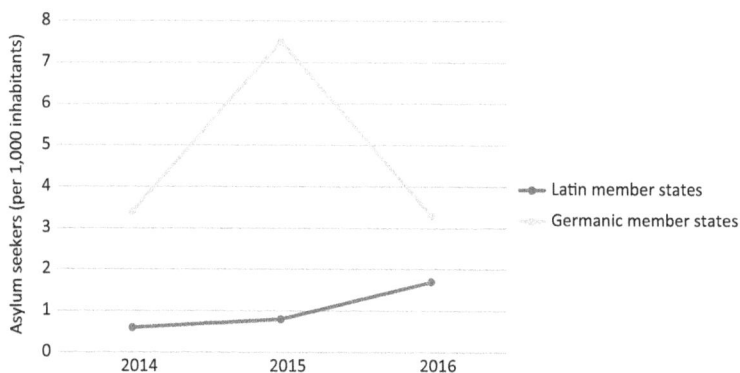

Figure 5.3 Number of asylum seekers.

Source: Eurostat – Asylum and first-time asylum applicants; own calculations.

---

21 Excluding the United Kingdom and Ireland, which negotiated an opt-out on this policy area.

Where this is unclear, the state where the application was first made is responsible for examining it. So how can it be that Greece and Italy (with an average of 1 and 1.2 asylum seekers per 1,000 inhabitants in 2014/15) lag so far behind?

To explain this we need to go back to 1997 when the heads of government signed the Treaty of Amsterdam. Under the treaty the (then) member states agreed to devolve certain powers, including legislating on asylum, from the national governments to the EU. This gave the EU the authority to issue legislation that the individual member states were obliged to comply with. The European Court of Justice is responsible for monitoring this.

The Treaty of Amsterdam has had far-reaching consequences, as became apparent when an asylum seeker in Belgium, identified by the initials M.S.S., appealed to the European Court of Human Rights against his transfer to Greece. The Court agreed with the plaintiff's claim that asylum conditions in Greece were so bad that the system was defective and that this was a breach of his fundamental rights.[22]

And so the plaintiff was allowed to stay in Belgium, thus paving the way for other asylum seekers entering the EU via Greece. Koen Lenaerts, the president of the European Court of Justice which adopted the verdict, responded to questions from a Dutch journalist who expressed concerns that Greece would take advantage of the ruling. 'I don't think so. Countries don't want to get stuck with that label. Because system defect means: total policy failure in your country.'[23]

In all likelihood, this eminent lawyer never got round to watching the Eurovision Song Contest; otherwise he would have known that Greece tends to take little notice of what other people think. Despite urgent pleas, financial support and threats, European Vice President Valdis Dombrovskis was forced to concede in a news conference that 'Greece seriously neglected its obligations under the Schengen agreement.' Spot checks by EU inspectors in November found Greece was failing to register arrivals properly, to fingerprint everyone, to see whether identity documents were genuine, and to check people against Interpol and other databases. A spokeswoman for the Greek

---

22 M.S.S. v. Belgium and Greece (2011, application no. 30696/09).
23 *NRC Handelsblad*, 13 November 2015.

government said: 'Greece has done more than it could to stand to its obligations. We expect from everyone else to do the same.'[24]

And Italy? How come so few asylum seekers are registered in that country while so many arrive there? Two Dutch journalists shone some light on the matter in a report highlighting the amazement of refugees after being rescued at sea. 'No coastguard, no fingerprinting, nothing.' A Syrian refugee removed from the train in Austria en route to Germany spoke of the advice he was given by Italian police. 'Use the same ticket and get on the next train.'[25] That is one way for a country to get rid of its asylum seekers without the need for complicated legal procedures.

In 2016, Greece and Italy gave in somewhat to the pressure from the EU (with Greece taking in 4.7 refugees per 1,000 inhabitants, Italy 2). Completely in line with game theory, most northern European countries reacted to the poor cooperation from their southern colleagues by taking in considerably fewer asylum seekers than in previous years. Because as we have seen if free riders are not punished the interest in taking part in a joint project quickly diminishes.[26]

The majority of asylum seekers were from Muslim countries. The experience of EU countries in terms of integrating these migrants has not exactly been positive. In his book *Germany Abolishes Itself*, politician and former Bundesbank executive Thilo Sarrazin revealed that in Germany the percentage of the Muslim population on benefits was more than three times higher than for native Germans.[27] As in other Western European countries, in Germany the unemployment rate among this group is considerably higher than the national average, they are overrepresented in the crime statistics, they underperform at school – in short, they form a problematic group.

---

24 BBC News, 27 January 2016.
25 *NRC Handelsblad*, 17 April 2015.
26 Germany was the only Germanic country to take in more asylum seekers in 2016 than in previous years. In the elections of September 2017 the coalition of CDU and SPD led by Chancellor Merkel was severely punished for this policy, with their combined share of the vote falling from 67 per cent in 2013 to 53 per cent.
27 Sarrazin (2016), p. 283: In Germany 13.6 per cent of the native workforce claimed benefits in 2007 compared with 43.6 per cent of the Muslim population.

The toughest aspect of these integration issues is the huge differences that exist between the Islamic value system and that of the host countries. For example, article 21 of the Charter of the Fundamental Rights of the European Union states, 'Any discrimination based on any ground such as sex, race, colour, ethnic or social origin, genetic features, language, religion [...] or sexual orientation shall be prohibited.' Residents of the European host nations where large numbers of Muslim refugees have settled take this for granted to the point where they believe these values to be universal. They are unable to imagine that there are people who disagree with these 'evident' truths. But nothing could be further from the truth. A survey of the opinions of native Christians and Muslims of Moroccan and Turkish origin in six Western European countries showed that only 3 per cent of Christians believed secular laws to be secondary to religious precepts; among first-generation Muslim immigrants the percentage was 48 per cent and among the second generation 38 per cent. These considerable differences filter through into all kinds of aspects of daily life. For example, 47 per cent of first-generation Muslims believe that Jews cannot be trusted while 39 per cent of the second generation hold the same opinion, compared to 8 per cent among Christians. Homosexuality is another tricky issue: 11 per cent of Christians said they would not be friends with a homosexual, considerably lower than the 62 per cent of first-generation Muslims and 47 per cent of the second generation.[28] Research in the countries of origin suggests that the views of the first-generation immigrants have already shifted in a 'Western' direction, with 85 per cent of Turks in Turkey saying they would not be friends with a homosexual, and the figure for Tunisia being as high as 91 per cent.[29]

Of course the issue of the relationship between men and women is also important if large numbers of Muslims decide to settle in Western Europe. Should a woman always obey her husband? In Turkey 65 per cent of men and women surveyed said that she should. In Afghanistan, Morocco and Iraq the percentage was even higher at

28 Koopmans (2014).

29 These and the following figures were compiled by Pew Research Center (2010).

above 90 per cent. The same picture emerges in relation to questions about polygamy, divorce, wearing a headscarf or veil and the right to inherit.

In short, the differences are huge. It is a head-on collision between two value systems. As a small minority (around 5 to 6 per cent of the population in 2010) Muslims initially tried to keep their opinions to themselves where they could.[30] The vast majority of their new compatriots were barely aware of these differences. 'Politically correct' politicians, scientists and journalists did their best to down-play the issues.

With some success. Until the heightened tensions eventually erupted in the form of terrorist attacks. After that, there was no way things could be covered up any more, only questions as to what could have brought these young people to commit such atrocities. And yet we could have seen it coming. Research conducted by the US PEW Research Center showed that 15 per cent of Turks believe that sui-cide attacks can be justified if Islam is under threat. In Morocco 9 per cent of the population holds this opinion. EU citizens responded vehemently to these desperate attacks, with as many as 58 per cent describing their attitude towards immigrants from outside the Union as a 'total negative'.[31]

Reactions to this confrontation with the newcomers varied widely in the various Western European countries. I will discuss three examples.

France

In France the debate about the integration of Muslim immigrants erupted in October 1989 when three Muslim pupils were expelled from school in Creil for breaking school regulations by refusing to remove their headscarves in class. The churches and various anti racist organisations protested. SOS Racisme said that on no account should students be punished for their religion. Education Minister

---

30 These figures relate to 2010. In that year Muslims accounted for 2–3 per cent of the population in Italy and Spain.
31 Eurobarometer 85 (July 2016). For immigrants from other countries of the EU the figure was 35 per cent.

Lionel Jospin tried to formulate a compromise but found his path blocked by the philosopher Alain Finkielkraut and various other intellectuals.

> *Monsieur le ministre*, you say that exclusion is excluded. Though touched by your kindness we respond that it is permitted to forbid [...] In order to be able to think for themselves pupils must have the pleasure of forgetting their community of origin and to think of something other than what they are [...] otherwise it is a trap, if not enslavement.[32]

The battle about how secularism (in French *laïcité*) should be interpreted at school and elsewhere carried on for years. The liberal interpretation is based on the principle that all people – and therefore their religions – are equal. On that basis headscarves, as an expression of the Muslim faith, should be allowed. In contrast, the 'republican' interpretation says that everyone must have the freedom to choose. Given that Islam does not afford its followers this freedom, headscarves and other such religious symbols should be banned. 'No freedom for the enemies of freedom' is the slogan of this group.

In 2004, the French National Assembly voted in favour of a law banning all religious symbols from French public schools, including headscarves, Jewish skullcaps and Christian crosses that are too large in size. This was followed a few years later by a ban on covering the face in public places, including with niqabs or burqas.

A satirical follow-up to this debate came in the form of the novel *Submission* by Michel Houellebecq. In it he describes how the Muslim Brotherhood party comes to power in France when the Socialists are prepared to form a coalition with them in order to block the Front National. Led by President Mohamed Ben Abbes the new government is a huge success.

> His first achievement was a dramatic drop in crime: in the most troubled neighbourhoods it was down 90 per cent. He'd had another instant success with unemployment, which had plummeted. This was clearly due to women leaving the

---

32 Finkielkraut (2014), pp. 17–18.

workforce en masse – due […] to a large new subsidy for families […] The subsidy hadn't even added to the deficit, since it was completely offset by drastic cuts in education […] Under the new system, mandatory education ended with junior school, around the age of twelve […] From then on, vocational training was encouraged.[33]

Just hours after the launch of this critical novel France was rocked by a terrorist attack on the offices of satirical weekly magazine *Charlie Hebdo*. The Islamist gunmen who shot dead 12 people claimed that the publication had insulted their religion. This terrible act was followed by more attacks, the worst being those in Paris (on 13 November 2015, 129 dead and 350 wounded) and Nice (14 July 2016, 84 dead and dozens of wounded). Public opinion, already negative when it came to their Islamic compatriots, now turned completely against them: 52 per cent of French people agreed fully with the statement that the borders should be hermetically closed to refugees while only 5 per cent believed that most refugees would integrate successfully.[34]

The integration debate, which took another bizarre twist in the summer of 2016 when two dozen mayors banned burkinis (full-length swimwear) from their beaches, followed a different path in France than elsewhere. No other European country has laws banning headscarves and face veils. In no other EU member state does the chairman of a new government commission in charge of promoting Muslim integration say: 'No more regulation, but we need to say things as they are – that the veil means women's subordination, the refusal of cultural mix, a message that says "we're not like you." '[35]

When we discussed cultural differences we saw that France has a high score for the basic value of power distance. This means not only that the country's organisations are characterised by steep hierarchies but also that people pay close attention to power and how it is exercised. The 'republican' view on neutrality in schools

---

33 Houellebecq (2016), pp. 157–58.
34 IPSOS, Global Views on Immigration and the Refugee Crisis (July 2016).
35 Jean-Pierre Chevènement in the *Financial Times*, 3 September 2016; NRC Handelsblad, 5 August 2016.

and public places should be seen in this light. 'Everyone is equal,' say the liberals, but 'What does that mean for power relations?' ask their opponents. If non-liberal Muslims are able to use such fundamental rights to strengthen their position or, as Houellebecq imagines, even come to dominate, they do not agree with this. They refuse to be intimidated by human rights activists such as Asif Arif, who wrote in news magazine *Nouvel Observateur* that Muslims are sick of being seen as second-class citizens. 'You would expect the Prime Minister to say that the terrorists have nothing to do with Islam, and that he will do everything he can to defend their freedom of religion.'[163] Demanding freedom of religion without granting the same to others in return is something many French people will simply not swallow. In the Germanic EU countries such contradictions are less overt.

The Netherlands

In 1992, a Somalian refugee arrived in the Netherlands via Germany who was to play an important role in the Dutch asylum debate. Her name was Ayaan Hirsi Ali. In actual fact she was not fleeing the civil war in her own country, as she stated in her asylum application, but rather the marriage her father had arranged for her and in which she wanted no part. A friendly uniformed police officer gave her directions to the asylum seekers centre in Zeewolde. 'I asked him: "Why are you helping me?" and he smiled and said: Those are the rules.'

She had mixed feelings about the asylum centre. There was a lot of complaining, especially from Somalis who were not integrating.

> They weren't working. They had nothing to do but hang about the asylum center and cadge meals. There were a few individuals who learned to cycle, who were ambitious and studied and worked—I wasn't unique—but those people had no time to socialize. The others just chewed qat all night and sat around talking about how horrible Holland was. We were all facing the same confusion. We had always been sure that we, as Muslims and Somalis, were superior to unbelievers, and here we were, not superior at all.

Ayaan managed to secure a place at Leiden university where she studied political science. During her studies she also worked as an interpreter, not just at refugee centres but also at police stations, prisons, courthouses and women's refuges. 'I began to wonder why so many immigrants – so many Muslims – were there [...] But I was beginning to see that Muslims in Holland were being allowed to form their own pillar in Dutch society, with their own schools and their own way of life, just like Catholics and Jews.'

After graduating Ayaan got a job with a think tank linked to the Dutch Labour Party PvdA. 'In those days, especially in Labor Party circles, people were always positive about Islam. If Muslims wanted mosques and separate graveyards and ritual slaughterhouses, such things were built.' Ayaan had other ideas on these subjects.

> The Dutch government urgently needed to stop funding Quran-based schools, I thought [...] All humans are not equal at a Muslim school. Moreover, there can be no freedom of expression or conscience. These schools fail to develop creativity [...] and they supress the critical faculties [...] They neglect subjects that conflict with Islamic teaching, such as evolution and sexuality. They teach by rote, not question, and they instill subservience in girls.[36]

At that time (2001–2002) the Dutch, and certainly the left-wing parties, were not ready for such views. Integration issues were seen as transitional problems which would disappear in due course. This proved to be a misconception, as sociologist Leen Sterckx demonstrates in her dissertation on mixed marriages. Commenting on her research she said: '*It starts at the wedding.* One family wants no alcohol and no men and women in the same hall. *The other family wants the opposite.*' The small percentage of marriages between a young person of Turkish and Moroccan extract and a native Dutch person (around eight per cent of the total), is more likely to fall than to rise in the future. 'Nowadays young people from Moroccan and Turkish families meet lots of people of the same age with the same roots. They are therefore less likely to break away from their background.' The revival

---

36 Hirsi Ali (2006), pp. 190, 223, 243, 245, 280.

of religion does not help either. 'The new chastity means that more often the choice will be fall on someone close to home. By wearing the headscarf, girls are sending out the message that they are not available for trysts. The headscarf provides freedom of movement, enables them to have a career in education, but does not bring them emancipation in terms of relationships.'[37]

Progressive parties and newspapers gradually changed their tone in the integration debate. In September 2016, *De Volkskrant* reported on the civil defence force set up in the village of Oude Pekela where asylum seekers are not popular with the villagers. The newcomers were being accused of whistling at women and throwing beer bottles at police officers. The paper cites Hendrik Schuitema (28), unemployed. 'Around here we are all simple farm boys. We haven't been to college. There is no work here […] And then asylum seekers come into the village with their expensive mobile phones and gold chains around their necks. When they go to the cash point money does come out. And that grates, you see.'[38] What is striking is that the newspaper published the report without editorialising about populists, racists or other undesirable elements. Like politics, the press adapted to the changing mood in the country. In 2016, only 13–15 per cent of the population agreed or strongly agreed with the statement that the Netherlands should take in more refugees than was already the case; 56–58 per cent disagreed or strongly disagreed.[39]

Ayaan's clear, uncompromising tone was not appreciated at the time in a country where consultation and compromise are highly valued. This attitude is the result of the low scores for the basic value of power distance which we saw in the chapter on cultural differences. In this type of environment nobody is considered to stand above (or below) anybody else: we are all equal. No wonder that the immigrants, whether Muslim or from any other background, were given the same facilities as the native citizens. After all, they too receive benefits if they are unemployed or sick, a (rented) home, private religious spaces, own schools and sports clubs. Following the

---

37 *De Volkskrant*, 7 October 2014.
38 *De Volkskrant*, 19 September 2016.
39 The Netherlands Institute for Social Research (SCP), Citizens' Perspective 2016/2, table 3.2.

murder of film director and author Theo van Gogh (in 2004) it was the Amsterdam alderman Ahmed Aboutaleb, of Moroccan extraction, who had the courage and insight to state clearly what the integration debate was really about.

> There is no place in an open society such as the Netherlands for people who do not share the essential core values of that society. All those who do not share these values would be wise to draw their conclusions and leave. We cannot accept that anyone among us demands that we respect his views and at the same time is not prepared to respect the views of others.[40]

This is clear and understandable language that is more reminiscent of the tough French debate than the woolly language resorted to by many Dutch opinion leaders 'in order to keep it all together'.

Germany

On 27 January 2016 the German Parliament listened intently to an 84-year-old Jewish woman who was relating her experiences during the Second World War. Ruth Klüger did not mince her words. She believes that while ordinary Germans perhaps did not know about the concentration camps, they were certainly aware of the forced labour going on in their midst. She considers these people guilty. After the war she would sometimes return to Germany, and when speaking to some people she would make it clear that they had not done enough at the time. Ruth Klüger ended her address on a topical note.

> Since then, however, a new generation – no, not one but two or even three generations – have grown up, and this country which, 80 years ago, was responsible for the worst crimes of the century is now applauded by the world for its open borders and its willingness to welcome Syrian and other refugees with such kindness and warm-heartedness. I am one of the many onlookers whose response to this has shifted from bemusement

---

40 Quoted in Scheffer (2011), pp. 176–77.

to admiration. That was the main reason why I was so pleased to accept your invitation.[41]

These are the words that many Germans still crave to hear: perhaps not quite forgiveness but at least mitigation of guilt for the crimes of the past by doing good deeds now. In addition to the low score for power distance, which gives rise to the idea that all people are equal, it is this deep-seated feeling that is the reason why Germany acted so generously in the migrant crisis. Bernard Schlink (born in 1944), the creator of the private detective Selb, expects this burden to diminish with each generation.

> Already, it makes a difference as to whether it was your father who was in the SS, or your grandfather. Was it a grandfather whom you actually met, maybe loved?
>
> [...] Already, I see that my son has a different relation to the German past than I did. But even my two granddaughters [aged four and eight] will still have to cope with it.
>
> [...] They will have to learn where this anger comes from, that it comes from real wounds that still torment people.[42]

Atonement and a compulsive generosity explain the 'welcome culture' that astonished the world and which, if Schlink is right, will continue to play a significant role in Germany's relationship with itself and with the world around it in the coming decades. At times, this quest to feel good can be at the expense of open discussion. When the prepublication of Thilo Sarrazin's book *Germany Abolishes Itself* appeared on 23 August 2010 containing a critical analysis of his country's asylum policy, Chancellor Merkel set the tone straight away by issuing a statement that the work was 'not supportive'. A week later she urged Sarrazin's boss, Bundesbank president Axel Weber, to dismiss his colleague. The same day Sigmar Gabriel, the chairman of the Social Democrat Party, SPD, of which Sarrazin was a member, announced that he would be suspended. Two days later

---

41 Spiegel Online, 27 January 2016.
42 *The Guardian*, 16 September 2012.

Federal President Wulff (the guy with the low mortgage rate and the flashy cars) added his two pennies. Subsequent filming sessions with the author were cancelled and more obstructive measures followed.[43] Criticism of Islam was unwelcome and freedom of expression had to yield to this. The German public, however, took no notice of all the subversions. The book was a blockbuster: with over a million copies sold in a year, it was the best-selling book since the Second World War.

This hypersensitivity in terms of the asylum policy was also in evidence when a large number of women were sexually harassed by groups of male asylum seekers in various German cities on New Year's Eve of 2016. Anne Heyn, 27, arrived at Cologne train station with her boyfriend.

> Just before ten o'clock we walked down from the platform. The first thing I saw was a concourse full of dark-skinned men: Turks and Arabs. There seemed to be thousands of them. They stared at me. I felt like a cow at the cattle market […] Once we were outside we encountered more groups of men who stared at me and tried to grab my bum […] In the weeks following the mass assault I often laughed at what people said on TV. How could they say it was an innocent incident? How could they say it could just as easily have been a square full of German men?[44]

An open letter from German author Katja Schneidt forced an end to the hypocrisy of politicians, the police and the press, who at first acted as if nothing had happened.

> Dear Federal Government, I have to grant you one thing: you have made a good job of it. Your attempts to nip all justified criticism of the behaviour of many people seeking protection here in the bud with the Nazi cudgel have borne fruit […] We have now reached the point that we keep silent about such incidents […] They are by no means isolated occurrences […]

43 Sarazzin (2016), preface to the paperback edition.
44 *NRC Handelsblad*, 8 April 2016.

But you are not allowed to say so. Then you are a rabble-rouser!
A xenophobe! A Nazi![45]

The last epithet is the worst. For many Germans, criticism of
foreigners, especially those of a different race, is still too distressing.
It reminds them of the Nazi era; then it was the Jews, now the
Muslims. Never again! It is striking that Ruth Klüger made the same
link between the persecution of the Jews and the welcome given to
asylum seekers in her address to Parliament. It remains difficult to
have a rational debate on this subject, as Sarrazin attempted. Did
Ruth Klüger realise that many of the migrants are rabid Jew-haters?
That many view woman as inferior beings who they can do what
they want to? The mayor of Cologne, Henriette Reker (born in
1956), was among those who felt it best not to overstate what had
happened.

> The men who were unable to keep their hands to themselves on
> New Year's Eve have a different view of women. It is a view that
> was common in Germany 40 years ago. When I was 18 I regu-
> larly had my bottom patted [...] Many of the suspects had not
> been in Germany for long. We need to teach them how we view
> women [...] Refugees need to do more than just learn German
> quickly. Integration courses also need to focus on teaching them
> how to behave in our society.[46]

Henriette Reker downplayed the issue. In my opinion, value systems
that have developed over many centuries cannot be changed by
means of language and integration courses. Her comparison between
the position of women in the Islamic world and in the Germany of
40 years ago misses the point. Such a lack of understanding does
not bode well for the future. Several months later, after electoral
defeats in various federal states, Chancellor Merkel openly revisited
her underestimation of the migrant issues. She would no longer use
'We can do this,' although she did add: 'By and large we were on the

---

45 www.facebook.com/katja-schneidt/posts.
46 *NRC Handelsblad*, 23 April 2016.

right track.'[47] This attitude raises the question of how long it will be before Germany becomes a 'normal' country that stands up for its own interests instead of trying to pay off a historical debt by taking on more of the shared obligations than the other EU member states.

The European Union

In geographical terms there is not much distance between the EU and the north coast of Africa and the Middle East. Given the projected rapid population growth in that part of the world, expectations are that the migrant flows to the EU will continue to grow in the coming decades, even if the civil wars that plague certain countries in the region come to an end. The United Nations expects the population of Syria to increase from 18 million in 2015 to 29 million in 2030, with Afghanistan growing from 33 to 44 million inhabitants in the same period. Countries such as Turkey and Morocco show a similar picture.

So far the northern member states have shouldered most of the reception of asylum seekers. Greece appeals to its incompetence and Italy encourages refugees to travel on without registration. How many immigrants will it take to test the boundaries of tolerance in the northern states? Nobody knows, but by now it is clear that those politicians who take a clear and negative stance represent the opinion of a growing section of the population. This is also forcing the established parties to harden their stance. It is likely that this will eventually lead to the establishment of a hard external border around the entire EU. Experts are divided on whether this is a practically feasible step. Should it prove not to be, the people will insist on other measures, with the return to internal borders being an obvious option. In that case, scenes such as in Calais, where asylum seekers are prevented from travelling on to the United Kingdom, will also occur elsewhere in the EU. The European Commission has already made calculations of the extent of the economic damage that would result from the reintroduction of internal borders but, as was the case with Brexit, this will not stop people from demanding such a step. The cultural differences with the Muslim newcomers in particular are too

---

47 www.hln.be/hln.nl/34662/Vluchtelingencrisis, 19 September 2016.

great to prevent this. Demands are made of the immigrants in terms of language but also and especially in terms of cultural adaptations that they are unable to meet within the set term. At the same time, the native Europeans feel so severely threatened that they want to see their sense of dissatisfaction in relation to the migrant issue translated into concrete and effective measures.

Struggle for Power at the European Central Bank

The divisions between northern and southern Europe have been apparent in monetary cooperation for decades. The anger and power-lessness of the Latin countries vis-à-vis the all-powerful Germans surfaced in a conversation between the French President François Mitterrand and the Italian Prime Minister Giuliano Amato during a currency crisis in November 1992.

> Mitterrand: 'If there wasn't this interplay between European currencies, speculation wouldn't exist. The Franc nearly succumbed. It is intolerable. There is no reason why the policy of a state should be at the mercy of volatile capital which does not represent any real wealth, or creation of real goods. It is an intolerable immorality.' Amato: 'I agree with you.' Mitterrand: 'It has to stop.' Amato: 'That does not just depend on us. We need to go further down the road of integation.'[48]

We now know that these gentlemen's wish was granted. Looking back, I have to admit that I systematically underestimated the tenacity of the Latin politicians with respect to the creation of a common cur-rency. This stance dates from May 1979, when I started my career at the international monetary affairs division of the Dutch Ministry of Finance. Some weeks before that, under the direction of the German chancellor Helmut Schmidt and the French President Valéry Giscard d'Estaing, most EU currencies had been linked at fixed (but variable) exchange rates. The follow-up project was assigned to me. I became the local 'Mr. Euro' and wrote long memos about options for further monetary integration. It was quite alright to leave this task to me – a

---

48 Marsh (2009), p. 170.

young, inexperienced civil servant – because nobody, including me, expected anything to ever come of it. This proved to be a misjudgement. Since 1999 the European Union has had a common currency and a common central bank that formulates and implements monetary policy. Before that point could be reached, the Germans had to be reassured that the new euro would be just as sound as their beloved Deutschmark and that they would not be liable for other countries' debts. Chancellor Kohl was able to convince his reluctant compatriots, a majority of whom were opposed to the introduction of the euro in the late 1990s. In a speech to the German Federal Parliament, he affirmed: 'According to the treaty rules, the euro community shall not be liable for the commitments of its member states and there will be no additional financial transfers.'[49]

In addition to this no bail-out clause, the Germans had another arrow in their quiver. This was enshrined in article 125 of the Treaty on the Functioning of the European Union (TFEU)[50]: 'Overdraft facilities or any other type of credit facility with the European Central Bank or with the central banks of the Member States in favour of [...] central governments [...] shall be prohibited, as shall the purchase *directly* from them by the European Central Bank or national central banks of debt instruments.' The article prohibits the ECB from buying sovereign bonds from national governments in order to finance their deficits. Known as 'monetary financing,' it is a much-used economic policy tool, especially in the Latin countries. I introduced the italics above because the battle between northern and southern Europe that has unfolded at the ECB in the last decade largely revolves around the interpretation of this one word. I will return to this later.

For a while all in the garden was rosy after it became apparent that all the participating countries were prepared to meet the German demands. In turn, the Germans were prepared to make concessions; although they had by far the largest economy and the largest population, they were prepared to accept a considerably smaller weighting in the distribution of the voting rights on the board of the new central bank. Luxembourg was awarded 3.7 votes per one million inhabitants

---

49 Kohl, speech to the German Federal Parliament, 23 April 1998. Quoted in Sinn (2014), pp. 20–21.
50 Treaty on the Functioning of the European Union (TFEU).

while Germany settled for 0.02 votes. Germany, like France and Italy, accepted that its voting rights on the ECB board amounted to only 8.7 per cent of the total number of votes.[51] This concession reflects the huge mutual trust among European central bankers in the late 1990s; in most cases, the gentlemen had known each other for many years and had weathered many a monetary storm together. They were also largely in agreement that the German Bundesbank, with its political independence, should be the model for the future ECB. The Latin countries in particular had a different tradition, with, for example, the Banque de France being controlled by the Finance Ministry. This set-up meant that the president of the central bank was bound to follow the minister's orders so that politics influenced monetary policy. Most of the central bankers therefore liked the sound of more power and independence.

However, politics was to get the final word, as became clear in 1998 when the time came to elect the first president of the ECB. As the Dutch Finance Minister, Gerrit Zalm was closely involved in the process.

> All the presidents of the national central banks backed the nomination of Wim Duisenberg. Nevertheless Jean-Claude Trichet allowed the French government to put him forward as a rival candidate. That sort of thing is unthinkable to a Dutchman: in that situation you thank them for their trust but decline. There is a reason why slavery was abolished. The French have a different way of looking at this. When the president calls, you obey, even if you don't agree.[52]

The contrast between north and south is very much in evidence here. In Latin France, authority was strictly exercised while such orders were unacceptable to the Germanic Netherlands with its low score for power distance. This was the spirit in which Duisenberg, as a good Dutchman, led the ECB from 1998. With his colleagues on the Governing Council, he managed to maintain the harmonious

---

51 Sinn (2014), p. 34. In 2013, Germany had a 27 per cent equity share in the ECB.
52 Zalm (2009), pp. 356–57.

atmosphere that had grown up between most of them in the recent years of intensive preparations for the euro. The Frenchman Trichet summarised the proceedings in the slogan, 'We are a team, the chairman is the coach.'[53] Voting was unnecessary; close mutual consultation always led to an agreement between the gentlemen.

Duisenberg was succeeded as ECB president by Trichet, who proved to be an obvious leader rather than a coach. Nevertheless, Gerrit Zalm was content with his approach. 'Trichet turns out to be an outstanding successor to Duisenberg. He is continuing on the chosen path of a sound monetary policy and is by no means led by French politics.'[54] To his chagrin, former French Prime Minister Michel Rocard agreed with Zalm. 'Independence of the European Central Bank is a means to an end, to win Germany's approval for monetary union, but it is not the end of the story.'[55] These proved to be prophetic words. On 6 May 2010 the honeymoon period in the ECB Council was over.

In the autumn of 2009, George Papandreou had been appointed prime minister of Greece and had declared that his country's economy was in intensive care. In the following months, rating agencies such as Standard & Poor's and Moody's rushed to downgrade Greek government bonds. Yields on the bonds went through the roof. The Greek government could not afford this and a crisis loomed. Fortunately, French President Nicholas Sarkozy came to the rescue by declaring that 'European governments sharing the euro currency will help Greece out of financial crisis "if necessary."'[56]

This pledge caused no problems in France but set off all the alarm bells in Germany. Politicians and the media pointed out that the French president had – without discussing it – violated the no bail-out clause in the TFEU! This meant that the Germans were now at risk of having to pay for other countries' debts after all. The matter came to an explosive head at the Governing Council meeting of 6 May 2010. Was the ECB going to violate its mandate and purchase government loans of weak member states or was it going to let the crisis

---

53 Marsh (2009), pp. 208–9 and 222.
54 Zalm (2009), p. 359.
55 Marsh (2009), p. 206. Quote dates from 2007.
56 Quoted in Bohn and Jong (2011).

run its course, forcing Greece to leave the Eurozone? In the press conference that followed the meeting, ECB president Trichet denied that the matter had been discussed. A few days later, at the weekend, the decision was taken after all: the ECB announced it was going to buy Greek government bonds. However, it would not purchase these bonds *directly* from the government – given that this is prohibited under article 125 – but would do so via other parties (e.g. via a Greek bank that had bought the bonds directly from the government a few minutes previously). In so doing, the ECB used a back door in the Treaty to enable the Greek government to borrow money at considerably lower rates than would have been the case without this support.

Axel Weber, president of the Deutsche Bundesbank and hence also a member of the ECB's Governing Council, gave the following reaction to the press: 'The purchase of government bonds poses significant stability risks and that's why I'm critical of this part of the ECB's council's decision, even in this extraordinary situation.'[57] That is outspoken indeed for a central banker. Trichet felt obliged to launch a counter-attack the following day. He gave an interview to the German *Handelsblatt* newspaper, which tackled him on the violation of the spirit of the Maastricht Treaty. Trichet vehemently denied it. 'We cannot imagine doing anything that would violate the Treaty – not even for a moment. What we are doing is of course in conformity with the Treaty's letter. What we are doing is in full conformity with the spirit of the Treaty.'[58] He also pointed out that the decision had been backed by an overwhelming majority, with only Weber voting against. Not only the Latin euro countries but also the Slavic nations and the other Germanic countries had supported Trichet. The French view on this confrontation was expressed by economist Jean-François Jamet of the think tank La Fondation Robert Schuman a few months later.

Angela Merkel was accused of acting irresponsibly – i.e. of endangering the very existence of the euro solely on the grounds of domestic policy (opposition on the part of the press and a

57 *Börsenzeitung*, 11 May 2010.
58 *Handelsblatt*, 14 May 2010. The Maastricht Treaty provides the foundation for the TFEU.

major share of public opinion to the aid plan for Greece within an electoral context), before resigning herself to it at the very last minute and unwillingly in the face of her partners' insistence [...] and the risk of the collapse of the stock markets.[59]

The violation of a part of the Treaty which is crucial to the Germans did not even get a mention in this analysis – that is how irrelevant the French considered it to be. What is also striking is that only Chancellor Merkel is mentioned by name; it would seem that Jamet takes it for granted that Axel Weber had received his orders from her. While the ECB is independent in a formal legal sense, from a French perspective politics is still the decisive factor in important matters. In this case, President Sarkozy instructed ECB President Trichet to stretch the Treaty a little in order to rescue the Greek government. Because of the distribution of votes in the Executive Council this approach was accepted by an 'overwhelming majority'. Germany suffered a total defeat. Axel Weber stepped down a few months later.[60] This paved the way for Italy's Mario Draghi to succeed Trichet in November 2011. By now the era of consensus was well and truly over. Just one month after his appointment he implemented an interest rate cut. The *Financial Times* commented that 'Mr Trichet would have sought a stronger consensus on the council; Mr Draghi went with a simple majority.'[61]

A few months later, with the crisis on the bond markets spreading to Spain and Italy, Draghi took things a step further. Without consulting with his colleagues he announced that 'Within our mandate, the ECB is ready to do whatever it takes to preserve the euro.' It subsequently became clear that this meant that the ECB would purchase government loans of any problem country. Weber's successor Jens Weidmann pursued the German opposition role with verve. 'We shouldn't underestimate the danger that central bank financing can become addictive like a drug,' he said in an interview with German magazine *Der Spiegel*. 'Southern European governments,'

59 Jamet (2010).
60 With effect from February 2011; Germany's chief economist Jürgen Stark resigned from the ECB in September 2012.
61 *Financial Times*, 7 February 2012.

the magazine added, 'could misinterpret this as a signal that they can obtain cheap money without instituting painful reforms after all. German taxpayers would be saddled with additional billions in risk without having any say in the matter.'[62]

Draghi was aware of the Germans' frustration. Asked whether he realised that 42 per cent of the German population distrusted him as ECB president, he remarked coolly: 'That is a hindrance for our work. I will have to do more to explain our actions. We will start with this interview. But you always have to weigh the options.'[63] Indeed, he had taken stock not only among the members of the ECB's Governing Council but also among the government leaders and had established that the vast majority supported his policy.

The voting proportions changed when two years later the Governing Council decided to expand its purchasing programme for government bonds to 60 billion euros per month and announced its intention to extend the policy until at least September 2016. Now Weidmann was supported in his opposition not just by his compatriot Sabine Lautenschläger but also by Klaas Knot of the Netherlands and Ewald Nowotny of Austria.[64] Now a real Germanic bloc was in evidence. However, given the larger number of Latin countries who were moreover supported by virtually all the Slavic countries, the bloc was easily outvoted. Just as Weidmann had predicted, financial support from the ECB proved to be addictive. The duration of the support programme has already been extended a few times since it was first announced, the amount of the monthly asset purchases has gone up and they now include corporate loans as well as government bonds. Large companies that have deficits can now finance these via the ECB without having to pay the high interest rates they would probably face if they had had to borrow from private banks or on the open capital market.

This was taking things too far for Gerrit Zalm, former Dutch Finance Minister and by now Chairman of the Managing Board of the bank ABN Amro. Although he was a supporter of independent

---

62 *Der Spiegel*, 27 August 2012.
63 *Süddeutsche Zeitung*, 14 September 2012.
64 Estonia's Ardo Hansson also opposed further expansion of the ECB's purchasing programme.

central banks that politicians were not allowed to interfere with, he could not contain himself any longer. 'Draghi would do better to sit on his hands or start a card-playing club.' He feared the prospect of negative interest rates. 'Savers won't understand it. It will lead to dangerous situations [...] I advise the ECB not to go there.'[65] German Finance Minister Schäuble practically begged the ECB to make it clear that the current 'abnormal interest rate structure is only temporary and that everyone is working to end it as soon as possible'. He was also angry. 'I said to Mario Draghi [...] be very proud: you can attribute 50 per cent of the results of a party that seems to be new and successful in Germany to the design of this policy.'[66] Schäuble was referring to the success of the new political party Alternative für Deutschland (AFD) which was waging a successful anti-euro campaign.

The Latin politicians had finally got what they wanted. The Germans and their northern partners had become the requesting party, while the southern countries were able to force through a monetary policy as they saw fit. How could it have come to this? If the northern countries had made sure when the ECB was set up that they would have the ability to block Governing Council decisions they would have been less vulnerable to the ruthless political style of their Latin colleagues. Another matter for consideration is the composition of the Governing Council of the ECB. It is inevitable that the old guard will eventually be replaced by new members with new ideas. While during their term in office they in theory represent the interests of the entire euro region, once their mandate ends they go back home. Their chances of an attractive new post will undoubtedly be affected by the home front's opinions on their track record at the ECB.[67] For these simple and obvious reasons political influences

---

65 www.nos.nl, 7 April 2016.
66 *Financial Times*, 11 April 2016.
67 The American central bank, the US Federal Reserve, served as an important model for setting up the ECB. The structure chosen is the same, that is, a head office (for the United States in Washington) and a number of regional branches. For years I was a visitor to the Fed and wherever I was, I was always told, 'We're only talking about the national numbers, son.' At the ECB it's a very different story; whoever you talk to, within a few seconds it will be clear what their nationality is and what positions they represent.

on the ECB are considerably greater than was the case when the
national central banks were still collaborating in the 1980s and 1990s.

How long is this going to last? How long will the northern countries be prepared to finance the southern countries? I expect this will
not go on for ever. Power structures which are characterised by a persistent minority who never get their way, tend to be unstable.[68] André
Szász, former executive director of the Dutch Central Bank and the
grand old man of European monetary cooperation, saw it all coming.
In 2012, he wrote:

> I firmly believe that we have manoeuvred ourselves into an
> impossible situation and I don't know if there is a way out. The
> great danger is that we are on a slippery slope towards a transfer
> union, a monetary union in which countries finance each
> other's deficits. If you deliberately agree not to rescue coun-
> tries that are in financial trouble and then you go on to do just
> that, you end up with a bail-out union […] I think it is unlikely
> that the Germans will accept a permanent transfer mechanism.
> I don't know whether the Eurozone will end with a bang or a
> whimper. If the Germans say that they are pulling out, it's all
> over. It would be like the sun leaving the solar system.[69]

---

68 Scharpf (2003 and 2014) makes comparisons between countries such as
   Switzerland, Canada and Belgium, where the rights of persistent minorities
   are protected, and the former Soviet Union and Yugoslavia where that was
   not the case, contributing to their demise as political entities.
69 Szász (2012), p. 164.

Chapter 6

CONCLUSION: WHERE DO
WE GO FROM HERE?

Value systems reflect the collective mental programming of human groups in a distant past. In some cases this is constrained by the natural environment they live in. For example, people living in the low countries on the shores of the Baltic Sea and North Sea have no option but to cooperate given that dykes, embankments and other flood defence mechanisms can only be built and maintained in collaboration. Strong or weak, rich or poor – everyone has to chip in because one weak section of dyke means that the land of everyone in the collective is flooded. It could be that the reason why Germanic countries score low on the basic value of power distance goes back to this particular set of circumstances.

It is also possible that the reason for the Latin peoples' high scores for power distance goes back to the days when Rome was under threat from its neighbours and its leaders found a solution in attracting large numbers of immigrants to defend the young city-state. In order to preserve their power, they established a system of patres familias with their 'clients'. After the crisis was over, this organisational structure remained, along with the considerable power distance.

Such solutions to existential problems have consequences for the group members' attitudes to right and wrong. The result is a value system that strongly influences how members of the group cooperate in all kinds of situations. While the problems disappear, the value systems remain without the members of the group even being aware of this. The result is that right up to the present day, Western Europe is characterised by two cultural regions which differ from one another primarily in how members of each group view power distance. In the Germanic tradition, people who do not stick to the rules and agreements are punished in such a way that another time they will adapt to the group process. This kind of 'social punishment' is less prevalent in the Latin tradition. Here, people in power have a tendency to protect their own interests first and punish those who get in their way. The fact that such 'antisocial punishment' can be detrimental to the group's interests is accepted in the Latin culture.

In the contest between groups of cooperators, where solidarity, altruism and trust predominate, and groups of self-seekers, where self-interest and cunning come first, the cooperators will eventually gain the upper hand. In Western Europe we have seen how over the centuries the Germanic countries have managed to turn their disadvantage in terms of population and size of their economy into a lead. In the contest between people at an individual level, self-seekers tend to be more successful than those who are altruistic. In the context of the EU this means that Latin politicians often outsmart their Germanic counterparts. The consequence of this is, for example, that Latin countries take in considerably fewer asylum-seekers and that Latin countries cleverly take advantage of the greater creditworthiness of the northern eurozone countries to borrow money on the cheap.

Game theory teaches us that Germanic members of a group are only better at cooperating than Latin members if there is a possibility to punish free-riders. This possibility is virtually non-existent in the EU. For example, euro countries whose budget deficit exceeds the agreed limit of 3 per cent of Gross Domestic Product year after year get away with this. The agreements on penalising this treaty violation have never been implemented. As a result, the motivation among the population of Germanic countries to continue investing in common projects is dwindling.

How can the tensions between the Germanic and Latin member countries, which have been increasing for years and are damaging the popularity of the EU, be brought under control? Will the Union be able to survive, or are we set to revert to the old ways of each country for itself? The basis for the further development of the Union must be that the EU will only take over from national states those tasks which are beneficial to all member states or to several, insofar as they do not damage the interests of the others. In other words, the voluntary nature is key. In discussing the various policy areas I argued that this prerequisite will be met if the EU acts on behalf of the member states in trade agreements with large countries such as the United States, China and Russia. The same applies to the regulation of the internal market, which must not be dominated by cartels or monopolists. The examples of the major European truck manufacturers, US giant Google and Gazprom of Russia need no further explanation.

Conversely, the common labour market is an example where integration has gone too far. In this case, there is a contrast between the Latin and Germanic Western European member states on the one hand and the Eastern European countries on the other. In the United Kingdom this force field was a major contributing factor in the 2016 vote to leave the EU. But in other Western European countries too a considerable part of the population is frustrated at the fact that a large number of jobseekers from other EU countries are not only competing against them in the labour market, pushing wages down, but also entitled to social security in their host country. The attempts being undertaken to reduce the competitive advantage of many Eastern European workers seem to me a sensible way of lessening these tensions. This step backwards in the integration process is necessary to prevent Brexit from being repeated in other countries.

The contrasts between the Latin and Germanic parts of the EU are most apparent in the asylum policy and the common monetary policy. Immigration from the Islamic countries bordering the EU has already caused huge tension in recent years. Given that the demographic pressure in the Middle East and North Africa will continue to grow in the next decades, expectations are that the number of refugees seeking to reach the EU from these countries will continue to rise sharply. Only politicians who manage to convince the population that they can control this influx can expect to achieve future electoral success. The EU can only retain freedom of movement if its external borders are maintained. Greece and Italy in particular have proved unwilling and unable to control their sections of the EU border effectively. If these countries persist in this stance, there is a threat of national borders being reintroduced between the member states.

The common monetary policy, of which the euro is the most visible symbol, is another acute problem. The structurally lower competitiveness of the Latin member states compared to the Germanic ones – as we saw from various studies into corruption, position of the judiciary and the relations between the social partners – will not be tolerated indefinitely by the population of either cultural region. In the south people fear a never-ending policy of austerity as the price for membership of the euro while in the North there is fear that the huge flow of subsidies to the Latin partners will never end and never be paid back.

Mario Draghi rules supreme at the ECB, but even he will be powerless if faced with an electorate, be it in the north or the south, that rejects the euro. A solution to this issue could lie in a return to an exchange rate arrangement whereby national currencies fluctuate against one another within certain bands. Such a system offers scope for many nuances and can be adjusted flexibly if circumstances so require. Fluctuation bands may be narrow (e.g. 2.25 per cent as is the case with the Danish krone against the euro) or broad (like the 15 per cent in the run-up to the introduction of the euro). Such a system would essentially be a D-mark zone. The question is which countries would be able to keep up with Germany economically. If a country's leader, such as Mitterrand in France back in the day or Italy's Berlusconi, wants to pursue an expansive budget policy in order to stimulate economic growth, this can cause trade deficits and put downward pressure on the national currency. In this case the decision can be taken to maintain the chosen fluctuation band against the D-mark, but another option is to widen the band downwards. Such a measure would imply a devaluation of the currency in question against the (new) D-mark. This would allow less competitive economies to retain their independence and at the same time limit the damage to trade with the other participating countries caused by exchange rate uncertainty.

How could such changes be introduced? In democratic countries an election is the appropriate method for this. Political parties that not only declare that they will if necessary restrict the movement of people by maintaining national borders and reintroduce the national currency but are also able to present a plausible plan for actually achieving this stand a good chance of electoral success in all member states.

Current EU legislation provides two alternatives for countries deciding to pursue their own path. 'Opting out', also known as 'constructive absence', means that a country will not participate in certain policy areas. For example, the United Kingdom and Denmark opted out of the euro. In addition, the United Kingdom and Ireland were granted an opt-out from the Schengen agreement which regulates the free movement of people.

'Enhanced Cooperation' is a procedure whereby a minimum of nine EU member states decide to go for more advanced integration or cooperation within the context of the EU than the other members. An example is the agreement on the unitary patent; Spain and Croatia are not part of this agreement, the other 26 member states are.

If a member state wishes to invoke either of these procedures it requires the approval of a majority of the other members. It is not unthinkable that the Netherlands, possibly following a referendum, could obtain approval to leave the monetary union and reintroduce the guilder. Such a move would likely not be possible for a key country such as Germany because it would take away the foundation of the monetary union. And so each country occupies a unique position and the circumstances of the moment will impact to what extent certain ties can be loosened.

A similar line of thought can be applied to the asylum policy. If Greece and Italy, for example, refuse to fulfil their obligations in this policy area, a number of other countries could decide to establish their own external border and make a serious job of maintaining it. Under the current agreements, such a group would need to consist of at least nine countries, but if fewer countries come forward a smaller number could be discussed with the European Commission. After all, negotiating adjustments to existing agreements is a fundamental feature of the EU.

The great disadvantage of having smaller groups of countries like this is that it creates a patchwork of arrangements. A country may cooperate with certain other countries only in the single currency and with certain others on the asylum policy. This complicates the functioning of the EU. However, this disadvantage is significantly smaller than the alternative, which boils down to the union more or less disintegrating under the influence of a frustrated electorate. In that case there is a real possibility that Western Europe could split into two, along the lines of the cultural divide separating the Germanic and Latin countries. This raises the spectre of two antagonistic blocks with all the risks to peace and prosperity in this part of the world that entails. An imperfect patchwork that the majority of the population of all member states can live with is preferable to a legal straitjacket culminating in confrontation between two cultural regions.

Like neighbours in a street, the European countries are inextricably linked and it is in their interest to get along. However, the ability to take account of one another is restricted by cultural differences. Neighbours in the same street can agree not to be noisy and organise a summer barbecue but would be wise not to go on holiday together, let alone get married – that is taking neighbourliness to extremes. Unfortunately, the EU has fallen into the trap of taking cooperation too far and over the past decade growing sections of the population have been trying to convince their leaders of this. People are not rejecting European integration as a whole but do want to take a few steps back. As long as this desire is ignored and dismissed as 'populism' the tensions will grow with the risk that the European project will incur greater damage than if bold measures are taken. In light of these circumstances the objective of 'no more war' requires a change to the successful policy of the past 50 years that was aimed at 'more Europe'. Who has the vision? Who the courage?

BIBLIOGRAPHY

Acemoglu, D., and Robinson, J. A. (2012). *Why Nations Fail.* New York: Crown Business.

Alonso Arechar, A. (2013). *Antisocial Punishment in Spanish.* Accessed on 2 May 2015 at http//arechar.com/behaviour/anti-social-punishment-in-spanish.

Arkenberg, J. S. *The Twelve Tables, c. 450 BCE.* Internet Ancient History Sourcebook. Accessed on 29 August 2007 at http://www.fordham.edu/Halsall/ancient/12tables.html.

Baantjer, A. C. (1994). *DeKok and the Dying Stroller.* University of Michigan: Intercontinental Publishing.

———. (1997). *De Cock en tranen aan de Leie.* Translated from the Dutch edition. Baarn: De Fontein.

Beauvoir, S. de. (1977). *Force of Circumstance.* New York: Harper and Row.

Bede, the Venerable. (1969). *The Ecclesiastical History of the English People.* Oxford: Oxford University Press.

Benedict – The Rule of Saint Benedict. www.solesmes.com.

Boccaccio, G. (2015). *The Decameron.* Translated (from the Italian) and with an introduction by Wayne A. Rebhorn. New York: W. W. Norton.

Bohn, F., and Jong, E. de (2011). "The 2010 Euro Crisis Stand-Off between France and Germany: Leadership Styles and Political Culture." In *International Economics and Economic Policy*, vol. 8, no. 1: 7–14.

Bornhorst, F., Ichino, A., Schlag, K. and Winter, E. (2004). *How Do People Play a Repeated Trust Game? Experimental Evidence.* SFB 504, Publications 04–43. Mannheim: University of Mannheim.

Bossuet, J- B. (1906). *Politique tirée des propres paroles de l'Écriture sainte.* In J. H. Robinson (ed.), *Readings in European History*, 2 vols. Boston: Ginn.

Camilleri, A. (2005). *Excursion to Tindari.* London: Picador.

———. (2007). *The Fear of Montalbano.* Translated from the Dutch edition. Amsterdam: Serena Libri.

——— . (2007). *The Patience of the Spider.* London: Picador.

Casari, M., and Luini, L. (2009). 'Group Cooperation Under Alternative Punishment Institutions: An Experiment'. *Journal of Economic Behavior and Organization*, vol. 71, no. 2: 273–82.

Castro, M. F. (2008). 'Where Are You From? Cultural Differences in Public Good Experiments'. *Journal of Socio-Economics*, vol. 37: 2319–29.

Chaucer, G. (1951). *The Canterbury Tales.* London: Penguin Classics.

Costas-Pérez, E. (2014). Political Corruption and Voter Turnout: Mobilization or Disaffection? Barcelona: Universitat de Barcelona & Institut d'Economia de Barcelona.

Crawford, M. H. (1996) (ed.). *Roman Statutes.* London: University of London.

Davies, N. (2014). *Hack Attack.* London: Vintage Books.

Druckerman, P. (2012). *French Children Don't Throw Food.* London: Doubleday.

Elias, N. (1997). *De hofsamenleving: Een sociologische studie van koningschap en hofaristocratie.* Translated from the Dutch edition. Amsterdam/Meppel: Boom.

Erlanger, P. (2003). *Louis XIV.* London: Phoenix Press.

Evenett, S. J., and Vermulst, E. (2005). 'The Politicisation of EC Anti-Dumping Policy'. *World Economy,* vol. 28, no. 5: 701–17.

Fehr, E., and Gaechter, S. (2002). 'Altruistic Punishment in Humans'. *Nature,* vol. 415: 137–40.

Finkielkraut, A. (2013). *L'Identité malheureuse.* Translated from the French edition. Paris: Stock.

Forman, D. R., Aksan, N. and Kochanska, G. (2004). 'Toddlers' Responsive Imitation Predicts Preschool-Age Conscience'. *Psychological Science,* vol. 15, no. 10: 699–704.

Gächter, S., Herrmann, B. and Thöni, C. (2008). Antisocial Punishment across Societies. *Science,* vol. 319: 1362–67.

Grass, G. (2008). *Peeling the Onion.* London: Vintage.

Green, D. H. (1998). *Language and History in the Early Germanic World.* Cambridge: Cambridge University Press.

Gucht, K. de (2012). *EU China Relations.* China Britain Business Council Summer Lunch, London, 9 July 2012.

Guiso, L., Sapienza, P. and Zingales, L. (2005). *Cultural Biases in Economic Exchange,* discussion paper no. 4837. London: Centre for Economic Policy Research.

Hedeager, L. (1992). *Iron-Age Societies: From Tribe to State in Northern Europe, 500 BC to AD 700.* Oxford: Blackwell.

Hermans, W. F. (Revised edition 1971). *De tranen der acacia's.* Translated from the Dutch edition: Amsterdam: G.A. van Oorschot.

Herrmann, B., Thöni, C. and Gächter, S. (2010). Culture and Cooperation. *Philosophical Transactions of the Royal Society B,* vol. 365: 2651–61.

Hirsi Ali, A. (2007). *Infidel: My Life.* New York: Free Press.

Hofstede, G. (1980). *Culture's Consequences: International Differences in Work-Related Values.* Newbury Park, CA: Sage.

Hofstede, G. (1997). *Cultures and Organizations: Software of the Mind.* New York: McGraw-Hill Education.

Hofstede, G. (2001). *Culture's Consequences: Comparing Values, Behaviors, Institutions and Organizations across Nations.* Thousand Oaks, CA: Sage.

Houellebecq, M. (2015). *Submission.* Portsmouth: William Heinemann.

Jamet, J.-F. (2010). *The German Ethic and the European Spirit: Can Germany Guarantee the Euro's Stability?* Robert Schuman Foundation: European Issue no. 182.

Koopmans, R. (2015). Religious Fundamentalism and Hostility against Out-groups: A Comparison of Muslims and Christians in Western Europe. *Journal of Ethnic and Migration Studies*, vol. 41, no. 1: 33–57. Accessed on 5 April 2016 at http://www.tandfonline.com/doi/ full/10.180/1369183X2014.

Lemaitre, P. (2014). *Irene*. London: MacLehose Press.

Lewycka, M. (2006). *A Short History of Tractors in Ukrainian*. London: Penguin Books.

Liljegren, R. (1993). Animals of Ice Age Europe. In G. Burenhult (ed.), *The First Humans: Human Origins and History to 10,000 BC*. New York: Harpercollins.

Maddison, A. (2003). *The World Economy: Historical Statistics*. Paris: OECD.

Mankell, H. (2011). *The Troubled Man*. London: Vintage.

Mankell, H. (2012). *One Step Behind*. London: Vintage.

Markaris, P. (2005). *Deadline in Athens*. New York: Grove Press.

Masclet, D., and Villeval, M- C. (2008). Punishment, inequality and welfare: a public good experiment. *Social Choice and Welfare*, vol. 31, no. 3: 475–502.

Marsh, D. (2009). *The Euro: The Politics of the New Global Currency*. New Haven, CT: Yale University Press.

Martial – *Epigram 6.88* (Quoted in Shelton, J- A.).

Meyer, E. (2014). *The Culture Map*. New York: The Perseus Book Group.

Mortimer, J. (1983). *Rumpole and the Golden Thread*. London: Penguin Books.

Palaiologos, Y. (2014). *The 13th Labour of Hercules: Inside the Greek Crisis*. London: Portobello Books.

Pew Research Center (2010). *Muslim Networks and Movements in Western Europe*. Accessed on 13 July 2016 at http://www.pewforum.org/2010/09/15/muslim-networks-andmovements.

Rademacher, C. (2003). *Deutschland nach dem Krieg 1945–1955*. Geo Epoche, no. 9: 80–81.

Rand, D. G., and Nowak, M. A. (2011). The Evolution of Antisocial Punishment in Optional Public Good Games. *Nature Communications*, vol. 2, no. 434.

Rousseau, J- J (2006). *Emile: On Education*. Surry Hills: Accessible Publishing Systems.

Sarrazin, T. (2016). *Deutschland schafft sich ab: Wie wir unser Land aufs Spiel setzen* (7ᵉ druk). [Translated from the German edition: München: Deutsche Verlags-Anstalt].

Schacht, H. (1955). *Confessions of 'The Old Wizard', The Autobiography of Hjalmar Horace Greeley Schacht*. Cambridge, MA: The Riberside Press.

Scharpf, F. W. (2003). *Problem-Solving Effectiveness and Democratic Accountability in the EU*. Max Planck Institute for the Study of Societies, Working Paper 03/1.

Scharpf. F. W., (2014). *After the Crash: A Perspective on Multilevel European Democracy*. Max Planck Institute for the Study of Societies, Discussion Paper 14/21.

Scheffer, P. (2011). *Immigrant Nations*. Cambridge: Polity Press.

Schlink, B. (2009). *Self's Murder*. London: Weidenfeld & Nicolson.

Severgnini, B. (2011). *Mamma Mia! Berlusconi's Italy Explained for Posterity and Friends Abroad*. New York: Rizzoli International Publications.

Shelton, J- A (1998). *As the Romans Did: A Sourcebook in Roman Social History* (2nd edn). New York: Oxford University Press.

Simenon, G. (1966). *Maigret on the Defensive*. London: Hamish Hamilton.

Simenon, G. (2017). *Maigret Is Afraid*. London: Penguin Books.

152   THE DESPERATE UNION

Simenon, G. (2017). *Maigret and the Minister.* London: Penguin Books.

Sinn, H.-W. (2014). *The Euro Trap: On Bursting Bubbles, Budgets, and Beliefs.* Oxford: Oxford University Press.

Solé-Ollé, A., and Sorribas-Navarro, P. (2014). *Does Corruption Erode Trust in Government? Evidence from a Recent Surge of Local Scandals in Spain.* Barcelona: Institut d'Economia de Barcelona.

Staël, G. de (1813). *Germany.* London: John Murray.

Sterne, L. (1772). *The Life and Opinions of Tristram Shandy, Gentleman.* Altenburgh, Leipzig: Richter.

Sterne, L. (2004). *A Sentimental Journey through France and Italy.* New York: Dover Thrift Editions.

Szász, A. (2012). *Kleine geschiedenis van de monetaire unie.* In R. Janssen (ed.), *De Euro: Twintig jaar na het verdrag van Maastricht.* Translated from the Dutch edition: Amsterdam, De Bezige Bij.

Suleiman, E. N. (1974). *Politics, Power, and Bureaucracy in France.* Princeton, NJ: Princeton University Press.

Tacitus (2009). *Agricola and Germania.* London: Penguin Classics.

Vázquez Montalbán, M. (2012). *The Angst-Ridden Executive.* New York: Melville House.

Vázquez Montalbán, M. (2012). *Off Side.* New York: Melville House.

Vázquez Montalbán, M. (2012). *Southern Seas.* New York: Melville House.

Warner, C. (2001). Mass Parties and Clientelism in France and Italy. In: S. Piattoni (ed.), *Clientelism, Interests, and Democratic Representation: The European Experience in Historical and Comparative Perspective.* Cambridge: Cambridge University Press.

Wasserstein, B. (2008). *Barbarij en beschaving – Een geschiedenis van Europa in onze tijd.* Translated from the Dutch edition: Amsterdam: Nieuw Amsterdam.

Wilson, E. O. (2012). *The Social Conquest of Earth.* New York: Liveright Publishing.

Waal, F. de (2001). *The Ape and the Sushi Master: Cultural Reflections of a Primatologist.* New York: Basic Books.

Yu Chen (2015). *EU-China Solar Panels Trade Dispute: Settlement and Challenges to the EU.* Brussels: European Institute for Asian Studies.

Zalm, G. (2009). *De romantische boekhouder.* Translated from the Dutch edition: Amsterdam: Balans.

INDEX

www.ingramcontent.com/pod-product-compliance
Lightning Source LLC
Chambersburg PA
CBHW020613270326
41927CB00005B/315